Cornwall and the Great War

Perspectives on Conflict and Place

Edited by Garry Tregidga

and Thomas Fidler

Cornish Studies

Third Series

Volume 3

ICS Associates

First published in 2018 by
ICS Associates,
Institute of Cornish Studies,
University of Exeter,
Penryn Campus, Penryn
Cornwall
TR10 9FE

Worldwide Distribution and Sales by:

Create Space
Amazon Books
5 Rue Plaetis, L-23338, Luxembourg
www.createspace.com
www.amazon.co.uk

International sales and permission contact:
Amazon

ISBN: 9781791596019

INSTITUTE OF CORNISH STUDIES
FONDYHANS STUDHYANSOW KERNEWEK

The third series of *Cornish Studies* seeks to develop the educational work of the Institute of Cornish Studies (ICS) in promoting a greater knowledge and understanding of both contemporary and historical Cornwall. It encourages a comparative and interdisciplinary approach which is open to new perspectives, democratic scholarship and community engagement. There is a particular emphasis on thematic volumes and the dissemination of the findings of conferences and projects associated with the ICS. Contributions relating to the Cornish Diaspora or comparisons with the other Celtic nations and other small regions and states around the world are also welcomed. It is produced by ICS Associates and for further details please email cornishstudies@exeter.ac.uk

Cover picture: A patriotic illustration featuring the Duke of Cornwall's light infantry emerging from a Cornish pasty with weapons aimed at Kaiser Wilhelm II of Germany during World War one, circa 1915 (photo by Bob Thomas / Popper photo / Getty Images ©)

Back picture: Falmouth War Memorial, 2018 (Photo by Callum Robbins)

CONTENTS

Introduction   1

1   Indifferent or Simply Different? The Cornish Response to the Declaration of
    War in August 1914   7
    Melanie James

2   'I have now had a look at the land of "Cousin Jacks" and Pasties: Cornish
    Australians in Cornwall During the Great War   32
    Philip Payton

3   From *Meeting the Kaiser* to *An Tankow*: Imagining the First World War in   43
    Cornish and Anglo-Cornish Literature and Theatre
    Alan M. Kent

4   'Sweet Rosa Trethowan of Fair Constantine': A Cornish Poem of the Great   100
    War
    Philip Payton

5   Investigating the Blameless in the Economic Context of post-WWI St Just: 104
    Looking back at the 1919 Levant Mine Incident
    Victoria Jenner

6   'Served, Survived and the Sewing of Seeds': How Helston Remembers the   120
    Great War
    Froshie Evans

Notes on Contributors   126

INTRODUCTION

Thomas Fidler and Garry Tregidga

> It will be a hideous, long, grim struggle - not a matter of weeks but of months,
> perhaps of years. It will need all our courage and resolution and endurance to
> push it through. This we must all give - but our great object must be not only to
> win - but to make it impossible that such a struggle should ever again be waged
> upon the earth.[1]

These solemn words were written in London by Francis Acland, under-
secretary of state at the Foreign Office, at the outbreak of the First World
War. As the deputy in the House of Commons of Lord Grey, Britain's
Foreign Secretary, he was an inside observer of the tragic events that had
resulted in global conflict. But Acland was also MP for the Cornish
constituency of Camborne and the words were written as part of a letter
intended for his constituents and published in the local *Cornubian*
newspaper.[2] This example symbolizes the way in which the war operated at
both macro and micro levels: drawing in a wide range of countries and
empires throughout the world with an estimated death toll of up to 20
million but at the same time impacting on the everyday life of small
nations, communities and families.[3] *Cornwall and the Great War* brings
together a series of perspectives relating to different aspects of the conflict.
What was the Cornish experience at the time? How did it impact upon
notions of Cornish identity? What was the long-term significance of the
war at the micro level? It is not intended as the definitive study of these
subjects; rather it is intended to mark the centenary commemorations of the
armistice of 1918 from a Cornish perspective and serve as a catalyst for
further research.

As the Institute of Cornish Studies (ICS hereafter) pursues its 'Global
Kernow' objectives, we cannot ignore the long-term significance of this
particular conflict. These essays engage with the War in a number of ways;
the response to the outbreak, the conflict itself, developments at home, and
the continued commemorative and 'collective memory' associated with the
conflict. But before considering the third volume of the series it is useful to
consider the wider academic context. The University of Birmingham's War
Studies department recently reinvented itself as a school of 'Military
History Plus... covering topics that are normally associated with
'traditional' military history... but also matters such as the organisation of

Armed forces; 'home fronts'; the impact of war on politics and society; the literature of war; law and ethics – and indeed many other things... seeking to demonstrate the breadth and diversity of War Studies whilst keeping the history of war at its core'.[4] What is evident from the existence of entire departments dedicated to the study of War is the breadth of the subject material available, but there is a shift in the focus from the militaristic element to the social, economic and political histories associated with conflicts. Echoes of this approach can be seen in recent years in the case of historical research on Cornwall. Stuart Dalley, for example, explored reactions to the outbreak of the war in the second series of *Cornish Studies.* He pointed to an initial reluctance to embrace the war effort that was demonstrated in low recruitment figures and this attitude was particularly the case in mid-Cornwall because many workers in the Clay industry felt alienated as a result of the government's decision to bring in police reinforcements from outside the region to defeat the clay strikers in 1913.[5] Pete London's *Cornwall in the First World War* looked at the conflict in relation to both the armed services and the home front and produced a book with numerous digestible facts and pictorial references just a year before the start of the centenary commemorations. But by London's own admission the study provides just a 'glimpse of Cornish life a hundred years ago'.[6] Robert K. John's fascinating study of the Cornish miners of the 251st tunnelling company of the Royal Engineers also provides previous unexplored narratives of Cornwall's contributions to the war effort in a more traditional study of warfare techniques.[7] This was similar to the approach taken by Everard Wyrall in *History of the Duke of Cornwall's Light Infantry 1914-1919*, for which the microhistorical lens was not Cornwall as such, but certainly the regiment that many Cornish people regarded as their own army.[8] Dissemination of research into this period has not been restricted to the conventional mediums of books and articles. In 2015 a group of student researchers led by John Ault at the ICS produced *Falmouth and the Great War* with Louis Allen as the presenter. Harnessing the power of the moving image the film combined the perspectives of leading historians on wider aspects of the conflict with detailed research on the individual experiences of servicemen associated with the town who lost their lives in war zones throughout the world.[9]

Cornwall and the Great War seeks to extend this debate in a number of key areas. Melanie James provides the first contribution to the volume with a study based on her MA research on the Cornish response to the outbreak of the war. There has been a tendency to focus on the growing interest in the Celtic identity of Cornwall in the early twentieth century with studies on the activities of early Revivalists like Henry Jenner in relation to the Duchy's ancient language and culture.[10] But James reminds us that this was also the age of British Imperialism and highlights the way in which state propaganda operated in Cornwall and other parts of the United Kingdom putting the official focus firmly on the macro identity of Britain and the Empire. Philip Payton then points to the global nature of Cornwall's involvement with a chapter that considers the wartime experiences of Australian armed servicemen of Cornish descent. He explores the personal stories of a group of soldiers who returned briefly to the Homeland from the frontline and in the process gives us real insight into perceptions of 'Cornishness' both at home and abroad at this time. A cultural perspective is also to the fore with Alan Kent's detailed account of the war and literature. In a wide-ranging survey Kent explores the work of novelists, poets and other literary figures whose work was influenced by the conflict both at the time and down to the present. As part of this process he looks at the relative neglect by New Cornish Studies of the Great War and highlights the fascinating story of Robert Walling's wartime magazine *An Houlsehas,* which was written in the Cornish language and even included a feature on the British tank.[11] A literary perspective is also provided by Payton who profiles the life of Richard John Noall of St Ives, who served in the Royal Garrison Artillery in the First World War and became a bard of Gorsedd Kernow in 1929. Noall was also a poet and the profile concludes with a wartime poem entitled 'Sweet Rosa Trethowan of Fair Constantine'. The penultimate chapter by Victoria Jenner shows that the Armistice did not mark an automatic return to normality. She looks at the tragic story of the Levant mine disaster in the following year when 31 miners lost their lives including some ex-servicemen who had survived the Great War. For Jenner the 'proximity' of the war shaped both practical and emotional responses to the event as the local community struggled to look to the future. Finally, a review article by Froshie Evans brings our story up to the present. Over the past few years it has been a time of renewed reflection on the conflict with public engagement projects throughout Britain. Cornwall is no exception with such initiatives as *100 Faces 100 Stories* coordinated by Jo Mattingly on behalf of the Cornish Museums Group and the Cornish Archives Network, while this has been complemented at the parish level by a multitude of exhibitions and publications.[12] Evans looks at a case study of commemorations in Helston and in the process highlights how many of these initiatives have been dependent on the drive and enthusiasm of particular individuals.

But there are many other subjects that have not been covered in this book and their absence raises the potential for further research. For example, in relation to political history the war has been seen by some scholars as being the crucial factor in the decline of Liberalism and the rise of Labour in Britain.[13] What was its impact in Cornwall where the Liberal party was able to survive as the dominant political force with victories in every constituency in the elections of 1923 and 1929? From an economic perspective Norikaze Kudo's research into Cornish tin mining after 1918 starts to build on John Rowe's pioneering article written back in 1975.[14] But there is still a case for more in-depth work specifically on the war years in relation to mining let alone the wider economy in relation to other specific sectors like munitions, agriculture and tourism. In relation to war and the Celtic Revival scholars can build on the early 1900s, a period which was clearly to the fore in publications like the 1997 volume of *Cornish Studies,*[15] by looking at the impact of the war years particularly given the points noted by Kent in this volume. Above all, there is an argument for a future research project that explores the wider impact of war on Cornwall and the Cornish through time. Studies by Mark Stoyle have highlighted Cornish particularism and the Duchy's practical importance during the so-called Civil War period of the 1640s. Similarly, Cornwall's strategic position in the past is reflected in sixteenth century fortifications like Pendennis Castle and St Mawes Castle, a tradition of participation in the armed forces notably through the Royal Navy and the significance for British and American military operations of RAF St Mawgan from the 1940s onwards. Other historical periods such as the French Revolution and the Second World War could similarly be covered by such a project from a Cornish angle.[16] Sheffield's *War Studies Reader* stretching through time from the Early Modern to 'the present day and beyond' is a model that could be usefully applied.[17] Indeed, by linking the military and home front dimensions of conflict it is envisaged that *Cornwall and the Great War* can therefore assist in developing new directions for Cornish Studies.

NOTES AND REFERENCES

[1] *The Cornubian,* 13 August 1914.

[2] For further discussion of Acland's wartime experiences see Garry Tregidga, *Killerton, Camborne and Westminster: The Political Correspondence of Sir Francis and Lady Acland, 1910-29,* Devon and Cornwall Record Society, Exeter, New Series, Volume 48, 2006, pp. 11-12 and 72-127.

[3] Estimates vary on the total number of global casualties as a result of the war. The figure quoted comes from the Robert Schuman Centre: 'The total number of military and civilian casualties in World War I, was around 40 million. There were 20 million deaths and 21 million wounded. The total number of deaths includes 9.7 million military personnel and about 10 million civilians. The Entente Powers (also known as the Allies) lost about 5.7 million soldiers while the Central Powers lost about 4 million' (Nadège Mougel. *REPERES, Module 1.0,* 2011)

www.centre-robert-schuman.org/userfiles/files/REPERES%20%E2%80%93%20module%201-1-1%20- [last accessed 16 November 2018].

[4] G. D. Sheffield, *War Studies Reader: from the seventeenth century to the present day and beyond*, Continuum, 2010, p.2.

[5] Stuart Dalley, 'The Response in Cornwall to the Outbreak of the First World War' in Philip Payton (ed.), *Cornish Studies Eleven,* Second Series, University of Exeter Press, Exeter, 2003, pp. 85-109.

[6] Pete London, *Cornwall in the First World War,* Truran, 2013.

[7] Robert Johns, *Battle Beneath the Trenches: The Cornish Miners of the 251st Tunnelling Company,* Pen & Sword Military, 2015.

[8] Everard Wyrall, *History of the Duke of Cornwall's Light Infantry 1914-1919,* Naval and Military Press, 2004.

[9] John Ault (Dir.), *Falmouth and the Great War,* Institute of Cornish Studies, Penryn, 2015. The film included interviews with 'notable First World War and naval historians: Professor Eric Grove (Liverpool Hope), Professor Jerry de Groot (St, Andrews), Professors Richard Toye and Philip Payton (University of Exeter) as well as Hugo White (Official historian of the Duke of Cornwall's Light Infantry)'. https://vimeo.com/131974392 [last accessed 15 November 2018].

[10] For an example of research relating to Henry Jenner and the Celtic Revival see Philip Payton (ed.), *Cornish Studies 19,* University of Exeter Press, Exeter, 2011.

[11] For further discussion of Walling and his magazine see Ann Trevenen Jenkin and Stephen Gadd (eds. and trs.), *Scryfer: Robert Victor Walling 1895-1976, Bard and Journalist,* Gorsedh Kernow and the Cornish Language Board, Cornwall, 2016.

[12] For further information on *100 Faces 100 Stories: Cornish Collections Illuminating the First World War* see www.100firstworldwarstories.co.uk/ [last accessed 30 November 2018]. For a good example of a study of a Cornish parish during the conflict see the work of the St Enoder First World War Project that recently resulted in Dick Cole and Ann Reynolds, *Trusting Fully Trusting: Remembering the men of Fraddon, Indian Queens, St Columb Road and Summercourt who lost their lives in the First World War,* St Enoder Parish Council, 2018.

[13] The classic advocate of the war being responsible for the rise of Labour was Trevor Wilson, *The Downfall of the Liberal Party, 1914-1935,* London, 1966. For an introduction to wartime Cornish politics, at least in the Camborne constituency, see Tregidga, *Killerton, Camborne and Westminster,* 2006.

[14] Norikazu Kudo, 'Tin Mining in Cornwall during the Inter-War Years 1918-38: A Chronology of Responses to the Changing Market Conditions' in Keio Business Review, No. 50, 2015, pp. 25-53. See also John Rowe, 'Declining Years of Cornish Tin Mining' in Jeffrey Porter (ed.), *Education and Labour in the South West,* Exeter Papers in Economic History, Exeter, 1975.

[15] Philip Payton (ed.), *Cornish Studies: Five,* Second Series, University of Exeter Press, Exeter, 1997.

[16] A possible model is 'Wales and the French Revolution', which is a recent project hosted by the Centre for Advanced Welsh and Celtic Studies at the University of Wales and funded by the AHRC that focused on the notion of a distinctive Welsh perspective to the revolution. www.frenchrevolution.wales.ac.uk/en/index.php [last accessed 15 November 2018].

[17] Sheffield, *War Studies Reader,* 2010.

INDIFFERENT OR JUST DIFFERENT?
THE CORNISH RESPONSE TO THE
DECLARATION OF WAR IN AUGUST 1914[1]

Melanie James

INTRODUCTION

An enthusiastic nationwide response to the call to arms in August 1914 has passed into the nation's collective memory, popularly labelled the result of overwhelming patriotism, fuelled by decades of imperialist propaganda which had come to infuse every aspect of late Victorian and Edwardian daily life. There is, however, continuing debate as to whether such enthusiasm really was so widespread, and whether patriotism was indeed the key motivator of voluntary enlistment across the nation.[2] In the case of Cornwall, there is evidence to suggest, that recruitment was not high, and there may even have been a general sense of indifference to the declaration of war.[3] This article re-examines prevailing theories about the pervasion of pre-war imperialism and looks at the extent to which it was woven into the fabric of Cornish life and its impact on the Cornish Edwardian; demonstrating how the appeal of Empire was more to usage and habit than to intellect as the imperialists sought to encourage the absorption of its importance into everyday lives.[4] It explores whether pre-war imperial propaganda significantly influenced patriotic sentiment encouraging voluntary enlistment in Cornwall in 1914. The article thus aims to determine the degree to which the Empire and the explicit implication to defend it had become an omnipresent cultural facet of everyday Cornish life by August 1914. The article also seeks to give fresh insight into Cornwall's early contribution to the war effort examining the county's response to the declaration of war and charting the nature of that response until mid-1915 in order to compile a comprehensive portrait of Cornwall's contribution to the nation's early call to arms. It seeks to cast further light on what persuaded Cornishmen to leave home to fight a war they had not expected against a nation they did not perceive as an enemy in a land which was not their own.

THE EMPIRE IMPERILLED

The late Victorian era saw increasing threats to the stability of Britain and its Empire from both domestic and international quarters. Internal social unrest and calls for social change were widespread. Mounting internal strife, manifested in riotous demonstrations and strikes, throughout the country, including the 1913 China Clay strike in Cornwall, became increasingly violent in the early 1900s, continuing unabated until the outbreak of the First World War.[5] Political instability in Europe and increasing trade competition from Germany, along with the latter's growing military and naval strength since unification in 1871, led to real fears of invasion, undermining Britain's sense of global naval supremacy.[6] Such concerns, combined with the growth of the USA and a militarily rejuvenated Japan, and the painful lessons of the Boer War at the turn of the century, all served to expose the 'weary Titan' and undermine Britain's global hegemony.[7]

Imperialists recognised that Social Darwinism, a relatively new concept, meant that the 'survival of the fittest' could also apply to nations. They drew parallels with fallen ancient empires and warned of the risks to the British Empire if lessons were not learned.[8] Against this backdrop a broader-based imperialism came to be encouraged. It was imperative that the working classes recognised the magnitude of the crisis and understood their duty to defend their Empire and the English way of life. The Empire thus came to be 'injected into British culture in a more profound way than ever before'.[9] The working class was persuaded to take pride in the superiority of the English race as a special breed and to recognise the importance of their own role. Through the imperial connection, 'domestic under-classes could become imperial over-classes' and feel part of a national enterprise which would lead to social unity and a generation of citizens conscious of their imperial identities, prepared to serve nation and Empire, defend them, and if necessary, die for them.[10]

CONSTRUCTING IDENTITY: ENGLISHNESS AND EMPIRE

The creation of a powerful national identity thus became of paramount importance at this time to the development of voluntary nationalism.[11] An *Anglocentric* version of British history, the predominance of Englishness over Britishness, was nurtured to act as a social adhesive. The Empire was perceived as British, but virility, heroism and justice, appropriated as innate national values and characteristics, were proclaimed English.[12] National myths were created to instil feelings of pride and encourage loyalty. English values were developed based on ancient heroes. Legends, such as King Arthur and Robin Hood were used to promote ideals of chivalry to subvert domestic tension, underlining the child's connection with the nation's heroic past and implying his obligation to its future.[13] Such an ideology created a national purpose. Implicit was the expectation that certain values, such as heroism, duty, bravery and justice, should be nurtured to help shape a common national identity. The Briton was encouraged to play the game and live by an exemplary code of conduct, represented by 'renewed militarism, a devotion to royalty, and worship of national heroes'.[14]

But various factors separated the people, such as region, religion and gender, as well as the urban-rural divide, such that public opinion was not uniform in its view of the Empire. Different classes related to it in vastly different ways.[15] The British saw their Empire *on their own terms* through the prism of their class and status system, with the working class relatively indifferent to it apart from the spectacle it afforded.[16] Whilst the Empire was largely outside most working-class people's consciousness, simply knowing that Britain ruled an Empire might have made people proud such that they may have harboured imperial feelings unwittingly.[17]

The Cornish however were undoubtedly aware of the extent of the British Empire. The collapse of Cornwall's mining industry in the 1860s was followed by widespread emigration to the colonies. Those without work sought a better life abroad. There was no deep affinity to England.[18] Between 1861 and 1900 74.5% of males aged 15-24 left the county.[19] Diaries and letters attest to a bond between Cornwall and the far corners of the globe.[20] A.L. Rowse, the prominent Cornish historian, recalled the particular Cornish affinity with South Africa, 'that distant land ... At home people knew what was going on in South Africa often rather better than what was happening 'up the country'.[21] Cornish newspapers regularly included articles entitled 'Canadian Notes' and frequent reports of Cornish gatherings in Johannesburg, deaths of Cornish emigrants in America, and even results of Cornish shorthorn competitions in South Africa.[22] Similarly, reactions to news of the Boer War illustrated how, despite taking place thousands of miles away and with no direct threat to Britain, public interest at home was captured nevertheless and there was much rejoicing upon news of victories.[23] Cornish school archives show how students were kept informed of the Army's progress. The Delaware School log for 1900 is just one example of many which records the several holidays given to enable pupils to take part in fundraising activities for wounded soldiers or celebrate victories such as Ladysmith and Mafeking.[24]

Notions of nationhood and imperial superiority were further encouraged around the country by means of spectacular naval exhibitions, celebrating nation and Navy in ways 'almost entirely removed from their functional origins'[25] to play to both national and international audiences.[26] Such spectacles acted as a theatre of identities as much as one of power and might, underlining the importance of the Navy's cultural role in making British identity the most prestigious, and which, on the world map, provided a symbolic link between far-flung colonies and the mother country, such that John Fisher, First Lord of the Admiralty, could justifiably claim 'the Empire floats on the Royal Navy'.[27]

The Cornish had a particular affinity with the Navy, sending their men to it and the Naval Reserve in huge numbers. Men from Cornwall and Devon at one time made up two-thirds of the Royal Navy's total manpower.[28] One Major Bawden of the Duke of Cornwall's Light Infantry (DCLI) remarked 'To the Navy, Cornwall sent eight men for one in any other county'.[29] And Sir Arthur Quiller-Couch, the eminent Cornish writer recorded how Cornish shore-dwellers were used to 'the sight of small naval craft in flotillas or great battleships at speed-trial or gun-practice' and how 'A good half of the boys meant to enter the Navy when they grew up'.[30]

When war was declared in August 1914, men all over the country enlisted for myriad reasons. Letters and diaries of Cornish volunteers show how allegiance to their local community perhaps more than a love of King, country or indeed Empire was a key motivator for enlistment, but there was nevertheless sufficient awareness of Britain's position in the international arena to recognise the value of being British, and to decide that Britain was worth fighting for, even if the Cornish often felt quite distinct and separate from the rest of the country.[31] Men could not have enlisted for reasons of allegiance if they had not understood why they were fighting. At the root of their motivation was an increased awareness and belief in a larger nation and Empire.[32] It is posited that such awareness was the product of years of indoctrination whereby the people had been exposed to unremitting nationalism designed to permeate every aspect of their daily lives, inculcating precisely the right qualities for war: loyalty, honour, and chivalry.[33] It began at the mother's knee.

EDUCATING THE CHILD FOR IMPERIAL CITIZENSHIP

Education: A is for Army, B is for Battles, C is for Colonies ...[34]

The recruiting experiences of the Boer War in which the dismal physical condition of recruits had been recognised caused great concern about race degeneration which the Inter-Departmental Committee on Physical Deterioration declared in 1904 was primarily due to poor motherhood.[35] As a result, a powerful ideology of motherhood was promoted. Population was seen as power and motherhood was given new dignity. Working-class women were urged to see the continuance of the English race, nation and Empire as their foremost duty.[36] Children came to be viewed as the most valuable of imperial assets, and the mother as 'Queen Bee, protected and fertile, producing the next generation for the good of the hive'.[37] Schools for mothers and mothers' friendly societies sprang up all over the country.

Mothers were recognised not only for breeding and nurturing but also their early instructional influence. They could be encouraged to manipulate recreation to bias the mind in favour of a legitimised heroic interpretation of militarism via clothing, such as boys' sailor suits, nursery rhymes, stories, toys and games combining fairy tales with more useful information.[38] Quiller-Couch remembered his 1870 Christmas gift: 'a box of leaden soldiers, French and Prussians, with a large champaign of cardboard set out with mitrailleuses from which – even so young a friend of France – I peppered the helmeted Prussians with volleys of dried peas'.[39] Such instruction during formative years projected an impressive image of the Empire and a positive representation of enemy and conflict. Mothers could encourage competitiveness, manliness, rules and discipline in boys, and school girls in domesticity and child rearing.[40]

The 1870 Education Act, introducing elementary education for all, ensured such instruction continued once the infant left its mother's knee. Education was conceived as 'the most powerful instrument with which to inculcate ... values and attitudes that were thought necessary for the suppression of internal militancy and reinvigoration of society'.[41] Good citizenship was increasingly prescribed in the working-class schoolchild's identity.[42] The concept of 'citizen' rather than 'subject' became important to promote feelings of national inclusion and encourage the required sense of obligation. The classroom became a site of 'ritualistic national belonging' preparing the child for the life of a good citizen where Anglocentric familial and imperial values were encouraged and where images of Englishness helped promote the idea of the nation as a family in which everyone had their place and duties.[43] By 1900 it had become increasingly popular to stress that children, including those in rural and remote areas, were being trained for an *imperial* mission rather than a purely national one. Village schools were tasked with turning out *citizens* rather than 'hedgers and ditchers' preparing children for the 'battle of life which will be fought in all parts of the British Empire'.[44]

The introduction of History and Geography into the syllabus from 1900 showed how race consciousness was seen as the way to instil national pride in children for they conveyed a heroic national stereotype that was compared with inferior races. British imperialism was justified because other cultures were inferior and England was a civilising influence.[45] Text books referred to 'childlike natives, strange looking people with silly languages,' who 'would rather be under the rule of our country, than be governed by chiefs of their own blood'.[46] Teachers' manuals from 1885 consistently used legend to promote exemplary citizenship and patriotism. Accounts of battles and great adventurers were described in theatrical language accompanied by stirring illustrations, with pupils consistently encouraged to identify with the wider community of the Empire that their forefathers had built for them. Overwhelmingly, the role models represented were the soldier or sailor, such as Arthur, Drake and Nelson, all encouraging men to do their duty for England.[47]

In Cornwall, school archives, letters and diaries illustrate how the notion of King, country and Empire was certainly prevalent in Cornish education at this time. School lessons could be saturated with references to the Empire. At Harrowbarrow elementary school for example, in 1908, the Head was known as a 'Union Jackist'.[48] A school day began and ended with the national anthem, Empire Day, whilst not officially introduced until 1916, was greatly respected, and royal birthdays were celebrated. The St. George's Day concert programme included recitations of *The Charge of the Light Brigade* and singing of *Rule Britannia,* and children were asked to bring in objects from various parts of the Empire.[49] Rowse, at school in Tregonissey, remembered winning prizes of books for Empire League essays and publication of a story in *The Queen.*[50] One young diarist recorded 'On August 9th on the Coronation of King Edward VII, our mistress Tot had six kittens and we saved ... one and are thinking about calling him King Edward'.[51] In 1904 the County Education Committee issued strict instructions to ensure all teachers adhered to Empire Day protocol so that 'children waved their flags, wore their patriotic costumes, and sang 'Hurrah Hurrah for England ... from Saltash to Sennen and from Bude to Budock'.[52]

Although both boys and girls were schooled in citizenship, they were intended to take away different understandings of their duties. Boys were to fulfil them in a manly, patriotic, self-sacrificing manner, while girls were represented as men's dependants, confined to domesticity.[53] This is clearly reflected in the 1907 Cornish syllabus where Needlework and Cookery, including 'buying, basic hygiene and washing up'[54] were introduced to encourage girls to be better mothers. The Calstock Continuation School log book illustrates these distinct roles by titling a set essay 'Washing Day' for girls and 'Character' for boys. Yet Geography for both focused on 'England's position in the scale of nations, Naval Supremacy, and Military Defence,'[55] clearly ensuring both boys *and* girls were aware of the importance of the Empire and the need to defend it.

But while elementary school logs include myriad references to the Empire, militaristic themes and attempts to instil duty and obedience, there are nevertheless many more which illustrate that the Cornish schoolchild's curriculum was varied and not at all singularly focused on turning out mothers and soldiers. For example, although the first entry in one boy's exercise-book is entitled 'The Battle Field' a poem calling men to arms, there is no subsequent reference to militarism.[56] Similarly, songs learned at Launceston in 1899 included *Whatever you are be brave boys* and *the little soldier boy* but also *Chinaman, The Sun is Up* and *Merry Christmas Bettie.*[57] Delaware School lists *O! A soldier I should like to be* but also *The Cat and her Kittens, Ding Dong* and *Winter.*[58] At Kelly College, a public school, whose pupils tended to go on to university or enter the Army or Navy, the school magazine records old boys' progress such as 'Letter from Sandhurst' and 'Mids, life on a man o'war' clearly meant to inspire the boys to follow in their footsteps.[59] But at the same time, neither the Empire nor militarism were the sole focus of the college. The magazine records the college's many sporting triumphs and concerts which certainly included *Rule Britannia* and *God Save the Queen* but also *De Ole Banjo, I want to be in Dixie* and *Would you mind passing the salt?*[60]

The 1907 Cornish elementary History syllabus included British imperial expansion, but it also insisted teaching be given a regional flavour by references to local events and battles.[61] Ancient English heroes featured prominently, with references to Alfred, Drake and Nelson, whilst King Arthur and Trelawney, particular Cornish heroes, were accorded demi-god status, epitomising legendary champions but reinforcing a distinctly Cornish heritage. Similarly, the study of Geography included the British Isles, America, Canada and the West Indies, but also the physical features of Cornwall, a study of the local soil, crops, and birds.[62] Rowse recalled his exercise-book, with the arms of the Duchy and map of Cornwall on the covers, 'so much more familiar to us than the map of England' with information on population, towns, industries, physical features and distinguished Cornishmen.[63] Liskeard Grammar School's song was particularly rousing but at the same time encouraged pride in being Cornish:

We whom alma mater draws
From town and moor and coast
Hope to win her proud remembrance
As in her we boast
May she nurture generations
Of good Cornish men
Watching o'er the happy schooldays of TRE POL and PEN[64]

At Kelly, the subjects discussed by the debating society show no strong preference for militaristic themes: one debate argued 'That compulsory service is advisable in the army,'[65] another posited 'That this house believes in ghosts'.[66] Kelly's magazine included a review of Seeley's *Expansion of England,* and articles entitled 'A day in camp,' 'The Life of Nelson' the Officer Training Corps, a review of a lantern lecture on The Transvaal and current events such as The Dreyfus Affair and Fashoda Incident.[67] New books added to Kelly's library in 1899, such as *Gulliver's Travels, The Young Colonists,* and *The Book of Cricket,*[68] also illustrate the variety of youthful preoccupations. There is perhaps more focus on militarism and Empire than in elementary schools, but a host of other subjects is apparent.

Shebbear Boys College focused on 'men, ideas, and ideals,' the college motto being 'Ad gloriam per spinas'.[69] At the 1907 speech day the Head claimed that the college aimed 'to send into the world men of brain, muscle and principle'.[70] The college felt that boarding school was an opportunity 'to educate pupils all round, in character building, living together, tolerance and adaptability' nurturing a strong esprit de corps, all valuable qualities for military service.[71] Public schools evidently sought to inculcate leadership qualities and high ideals, but education in general was wide-ranging in nature. Even in rural elementary schools, pupils were encouraged to feel proud of the Empire but in Cornish schools, there was also a concerted effort to instil a particular sense of pride in being Cornish.

RELIGION: FOR GOD AND COUNTRY

Outside the schoolroom, via the church, Sunday Schools and organisations such as the Band of Hope and Boys' Brigade, patriotism was combined with religiosity and recreation.[72] Religion occupied a substantial part of the nation's life at this time. Its proponents were able to exert enormous influence on the thoughts and behaviour of the people. Chaplains spoke proudly of England as the master nation and the English as the conquering race.[73] Hymns and sermons became increasingly militaristic and patriotic, encouraging citizens to become good Christian soldiers and pledge allegiance to their country.[74] Christian voluntary organisations provided leisure activities with religious and moral objectives for working-class children, and church halls were built to provide venues for them.[75] Numerous youth organisations were formed, their deliberate aim being to combat the degeneration of inner-city youth and working-class militancy by containing and redirecting youthful energy from thoughts of discontent, building character and fostering loyalty should Britain's Empire be threatened with war.[76] The subjugation of the individual to the team in such brigades was easily transferred subsequently to regimental service. Again, the notion of enemy and conflict, and the ennobling characteristic of war, was implicit.

In 1904 church membership peaked at over 50% of the population in England and Wales, while in Cornwall, a Methodist stronghold, membership rose as high as 67.7%.[77] Methodism in Cornwall came to fashion every aspect of daily life, instilling a deep moral Christian code of conduct and exerting such a strong influence that the chapel became the main social cement, offering leisure pursuits which spilled over into working life. Rowse remarked how 'the vast majority went to chapel' with Sundays 'an orgy of church and Sunday School-going'.[78] One man's diary recalled how 'chapels were the hub of village life', another remembered how most social activities, including tea-treats and volunteer bands, revolved around the chapels and Sunday Schools.[79] Since Methodism was 'much concerned with the individual and his betterment', improvement, temperance and choral societies were very active throughout Cornwall. There were no rowdy music-halls as in other parts of the country.[80] Instead, brass bands and male-voice choirs generated a considerable pride in a Cornish separate identity. There were numerous Bands of Hope.[81] Its festival[82] was a social highlight, with children parading and singing temperance songs.[83]

The Boy Scouts were well-established in Cornwall by 1910 when Baden-Powell visited, but the county's various brigades associated with the church seem to have been more popular, signifying a close Cornish connection between religion and social activity.[84] One man's diary recorded his band and choir practices at the Wesleyan Chapel, his pride in his first Boys' Brigade uniform, and attending Christian Endeavour meetings.[85] The parish magazine of St. John the Evangelist in Truro recorded the setting up of the local Church Lads' Brigade in 1906.[86] It describes the Brigade's outings and annual camps where the troops paraded and said prayers but also enjoyed bathing, cricket, aquatic sports, rode donkeys, played in the sand dunes and participated in sham fights.[87] Clearly militarism and religion were necessary features of such youth groups but their activities also provided great diversion.

The county's parish magazines are full of reports of Sunday School treats for children and daytrips for adults.[88] The Bodmin parish magazine introduced a 'Men's Corner' in 1910 with subjects including bees, divorce, temperance, and socialism, but little mention of Empire or militarism.[89] Parish magazines refer to the many guilds which had sprung up, such as the football guild, which the rector encouraged to 'Play up' and the Choir guild, Needlework Guild, and Mothers' Union whom the rector reminded to 'do their duty to their children', directing them to teach 'obedience, duty and prayer'.[90] He also urged regular school attendance because of the 'sense of obligations and attention to duty' it instilled, because 'the most intelligent and sharpest young man will fail in life if he cannot be depended upon to be at his post when he ought to be'.[91]

The church's moral teaching continued through books held in Sunday School libraries, such as *Miss Irving's Bible* and *Doing Good* at the Gunnislake Bible Christian Sunday School.[92] Church libraries' reading material, printed inexpensively to secure maximum readership, again aimed to control the pursuits of the newly literate, reflecting the same themes as school books: militaristic and heroic legend accompanied by exciting illustrations.[93] Sometimes the only books in working-class homes were prizes for regular attendance at the Band of Hope or Sunday School.[94] Rowse remembered 'there were no books at home, not a single one'.[95]

WORK, REST AND PLAY

Much of the juvenile literature of the period, such as that of Henty,[96] a prolific author at this time, featured adventures in an imperial setting[97] in which Britain was seen as a civilising force, with manly fortitude and muscular Christianity the dominant characteristics and cowardice the most contemptible of vices.[98] The formula typically featured a young adult protagonist, the archetypal warrior hero, going forth into the thrilling world of Empire to gain his spurs in glorious battles. Schools and parents bought such books as prizes or presents, the message reiterating that of the schoolroom and chapel: Britain was superior to foreign cultures. From the 1890s, Germany's growing naval power saw it consistently portrayed as an invasion threat. *The Spies of Wight* (1899) marked the beginning of a spate of fictional anticipations of a future Anglo-German war.[99]

The growth of boys' magazines during the period was phenomenal.[100] Scarcely a story appeared which did not carry an action-packed patriotic message alongside rousing illustrations encouraging pride in the Empire. Empire-building was presented as courageous with violence legitimated as part of the moral force of a superior race. Low prices brought magazines to the working class, while the *Boy's Own Paper* was often distributed free or awarded as a prize in elementary and Sunday Schools. It was felt at the time that such reading material did more to provide recruits for the Navy and Army than anything else.[101]

Working Men's Clubs also provided opportunities for reading. In Cornwall, reading material available at the Tehidy working men's club illustrated the Methodist principle of 'the gospel of self-help'[102] as well as militarism and the Empire with such titles as *Engineering, English Mechanic* and *Royal Magazine*.[103] The Liskeard Working Men's Institute which had amassed 850 books by 1886 also held lectures on a variety of educational topics, such as 'the electric telegraph', 'America', and an 'anti-war lecture'.[104] The 1899 Redruth Literary and Debating Society syllabus shows a diverse range of topics for discussion, such as 'Weak Points of Darwinism' to 'Total Abstinence v Moderate Drinking'.[105] Exhibitions and lantern slides were also popular, covering subjects from 'Burmah' to 'Nautical themes' and The Navy League held lectures, one being 'Round South America and the Panama Canal'.[106] People were encouraged to take note of the wider Empire, but all as part of the Methodist principle of broadening knowledge in general. Whilst the Empire and militarism featured, they were but two strands in the rich tapestry of Cornish life. Methodism played a much more influential role in moulding Cornish minds.

Other forms of leisure, such as pantomimes, the cinema, theatre, and ceremonial pageantry, such as royal funerals, coronations, jubilees and Empire Day all played a role in spreading the message of Britain's eminence.[107] The growth of advertising also meant that consumables, such as postcards, cigarettes, whisky and biscuits could be used to promote militarism and the lure of exotic corners of the Empire, the Union Jack often prominent on packaging.[108]

Cornish newspapers testify to how people were encouraged to play a role in shaping the Empire:

> Men! You made CANADA
> what she is
> Come and help to make her GREATER![109]

Newspapers also reflect the new appeal of cinema at this time. Films at the County Picture Theatre in Truro in 1914 reflect the adventure the Empire offered, such as *The Heroine of De Beers Mine* ('An African War and Mining Picture'), *Captured by Bedouins* ('An Egyptian Drama'), *The Bravery of Dora* ('Another fine war picture') and *The Genius of Fort Lapawai* ('a thrilling Indian episode of the early days in America').[110] Rowse remembered 'the first moving pictures ... warships being bombed by Zeppelins ... It was just on the threshold of the war. We were very excited'.[111]

WAR IS DECLARED: THE CORNISH RESPONSE

On 25 June the first serious reference to hostility was announced in the *Royal Cornwall Gazette*. Although entitled: 'The German Menace', the article made no mention of any danger to Britain. On 2 July, it proclaimed that there were 'Battleships at Padstow!' Readers were not to be alarmed, however. Rather, they were invited to come aboard to explore, for it was the holiday season.[112] That Cornwall was in carnival mood in July 1914 is unquestionable. The newspapers were packed with news of agricultural shows, garden fetes, summer sales, rallies, festivals, and sports events to tempt holidaymakers.[113] There were more serious news items of course, such as Home Rule in Ireland, strikes, women's suffrage, and the price of tin but the atmosphere in Cornwall throughout July was decidedly merry.

On 28 July, the *Royal Cornwall Gazette* included a small paragraph announcing: 'Austria declares war on Servia' but the general tone of the newspaper was one of merriment.[114] As war loomed, the newspapers hoped for favourable weather as the Bank Holiday approached. On 1 August, the *West Briton* included features on suffragism and the St. Austell vegetable show. It did acknowledge the *continental* war but there was a more pressing concern: '... the weather is the most disturbing factor'.[115] Inside, it referred to the Territorials' encampment, free motor rides and sports activities, but also 'The European Crisis' and a 'Prayer for Peace' from the Bishop of Truro, leaving for Canada. Such was the mood in Cornwall on the eve of the First World War.

But just a few days later the *Royal Cornwall Gazette* headlines on 6 August declared that 'Great Britain accepts Germany's challenge, a fight for Honour, Truth, and Justice. England expects that every man will do his duty'.[116] From the tone of the subsequent text, it is evident that a *naval* war was expected and, in that regard, it was believed Britain was well prepared.[117] The newspapers recorded the mobilisation of Cornishmen in the Navy and Reserve in such numbers that it was feared the removal of so many men from fishing ports would have 'a retarding effect on the fisheries'.[118] The Cornish felt the war was 'a matter for the Navy,' and felt they contributed handsomely.[119] There was no indication of the trench warfare to come. On 20 August the *Royal Cornwall Gazette* still felt able to humorously recommend the best way to cook a German sausage as '... on a British Kitchener, use a Japan enamelled saucepan, Greece well with Russian tallow, flavour with a little Jellicoe, Servia (Help!), with little French capers and Brussels Scouts'.[120]

Little else now featured in the newspapers. Festivities and sports were cancelled 'on account of the dark cloud overhanging the country' and the 'scarcity of players owing to the war'.[121] Each column attested to the county's noble efforts as everyone rallied to the cause. Patriotic funds were initiated, Red Cross and ambulance classes set up, Belgian refugees were accommodated, large houses and schools converted to hospitals. Girls set about making garments and mattresses for wounded soldiers, and women's groups provided meals for troops.[122] There was some peace movement activity, but it was very limited and made little impact.[123]

And yet, by September, Cornwall stood accused of a poor response to the call to arms and by March 1915 Cornish recruitment figures were deemed to be so low that a recruitment march was organised throughout the county to encourage men to enlist. Yet Cornwall's low population, resulting from decades of emigration, meant that there were relatively few men in the necessary age bracket available for voluntary military service.[124] Moreover, agricultural work and mining, as reserved occupations, kept many potential volunteers from enlisting. Perhaps of greatest significance is that, given the county's sea-faring history and sea-girt status, the Navy appeared to be a more compelling option for the Cornishmen who did come forward. Indeed, there seems little justification for accusing Cornwall of apathy given the huge numbers already in the Navy and Reserve when war was declared, and newspaper reports detailing the great response when the Navy called for more.

The *Royal Cornwall Gazette* regularly published an 'Appeal to

Cornishmen' but noted how men had tried to enlist but found 'no place to sleep, no instructions to train' and that they had been 'asked to go back home at their own expense'.[125] Several spoke out defending the county including Major Stokoe (DCLI), Argus, (a *West Briton* columnist) and the Earl of Mount Edgecumbe who wrote that 'no county sent such a large proportion of its sons to the Royal Navy as Cornwall'.[126] The *West Briton* wrote of 'places in the county ... where calls for the army are unheeded by youths ... who are really anxious to join the navy'[127] reflecting Cornwall's sea-faring traditions, its pride in naval superiority and negative perception of the Army, for, to the Cornish 'the Army seldom came within their ken, almost never within range of their domestic concern'.[128]

But the official recruitment returns dated 12 November 1914 did not include Naval enlistment figures.[129] Similarly, The Statistics of the British Military Effort only provided figures for the Army and Royal Flying Corps. Any enlistment figures that do exist for the Navy do not denote the recruit's place of origin but rather his place of enlistment. Given the high number of Cornishmen who had emigrated in the decades preceding the war, the proportion of recruits from the dominions and the USA originally from Cornwall, or sons of Cornishmen, would indicate that Cornwall's early contribution to the war effort was, in stark contrast to reports, quite exemplary.[130] But without official data to corroborate this claim, it is very challenging to substantiate.

Nevertheless, Cornwall, particularly its rural areas, was deemed unpatriotic. Despite the endeavours of the imperialists to prepare the country for war, it is clear that, initially, many had no idea why the country was at war, particularly with Germany.[131] There is only one mention of Germany in newspapers consulted during the period January to June 1914, and no indication of impending war.[132] Similarly, parish magazines made no reference to Germany or the threat of war beforehand. One vicar's Christmas message to his congregation in 1914 compared it with that of 1913, noting how no one could have dreamt then that the country would be at war within the year.[133]

One reason for the slow early enlistment in rural areas of Cornwall was the harvest. Diaries attest to how it hampered early recruitment. One Private believed 'every active man wanted to go, but work had to be done and ... it needed more self-sacrifice, ... to stick to one's last than to throw everything to the winds and join the Army'.[134] One priest remembered that 'the harvest had to be brought in, and men can give little thought to war when they are in charge of a reaper and binder' but also that his church was crowded when war was declared.[135] One man who asked his farmer to keep his place open was told 'You needn't come and ask me for a job, you'll never work for me again'.[136] Farmers' work was crucial, one commenting 'many people forget that if we want to reap next year the work on the farm must be accomplished in the winter'.[137] Volunteering was actively discouraged for agricultural labourers.[138] Miners were to some extent exempt although many still enlisted. China Clay miners were regarded as the most reticent in Cornwall, but this was because of conflict in 1913, not war opposition.[139] At the same time, there were those employers who forced enlistment. Lord Levan of St. Michael's Mount stipulated that he would 'not engage any persons between 19-30'.[140] It was also understood that many men were engaged in Government service which was absolutely necessary for 'providing the sinews of war for those at the front'.[141] Some were rejected for health reasons.[142] But undeniably, there were also those who simply refused to enlist.[143]

While accusations continued, recruitment figures published in the newspapers and parish magazines nevertheless indicate a county geared for war. In October the parish magazine of St-Just-in-Roseland talked of 'troops which now number over 4,000'.[144] Newspapers also cited high recruitment figures for various towns and villages, such as 300 for Liskeard, 72 for the tiny village of Mevagissey, Mousehole 220, Fowey and St. Ives 200 each, Truro 800, Camborne 725 and 3,134 for South East Cornwall,[145] whilst Liskeard Grammar School was proud of its contribution of 31, 'very creditable indeed for a school so young as ours'.[146] Such numbers do not correspond at all with the figure of 1,122 (or 2.7% of men eligible for service) quoted in the official returns.[147] Even if recruitment figures for the Territorials are included, the official number only rises to 3,270 (or 7.7%) which still seems to bear little resemblance to the numbers quoted in county newspapers, but given 4% was deemed to be a high contribution, the inclusion of this addition makes a significant difference.[148]

Recruitment figures published in the *West Briton* on 17 December 1914 show that out of 217 parishes, 97 contributed over 4% of its eligible males, 63 contributed between 2.5 and 4%, and 51 contributed below 2.5%, which again suggests that Cornwall was not the serious offender it was accused of being. St. Michael Caerhays and St. Michael's Mount where the landed families were still able to exert pressure, had very high recruiting figures (15% and 16.21% respectively) whereas small agricultural parishes such as St. Levan (1.09%) had farmers exerting pressure on their labourers *not* to enlist.[149] Many towns and villages were recorded as having high enlistment figures, such as Latchley (25%) which, at the time, was deemed to be the highest in the country,[150] while residents of Callington, 'the blackest spot in England' defended the town's reputation with angry letters, one stating that out of a population of 1,700, 37 were in the Navy, 33 in the Army, 30 in the Territorials, 100 engaged in home defence, 17 medically unfit, and 16 with reasonable excuses due to family commitments, adding that 'if every other place had done so well in proportion, there would have been no need for so much recruiting'.[151]

Appeals for Army recruits appeared regularly in the local press. However, the Cornish had been taught by church and chapel to regard war as anti-Christian, so recruitment in 1914 *was* a delicate task. The challenge was to awaken the sense of private duty towards the endangered nation and contend with conscience.[152] Some letters attest to a strong abhorrence of war, but once it became clear that the church encouraged enlistment believing the cause to be just, the collective conscience was cleared, volunteering was deemed the Christian thing to do, especially once news of German atrocities reached home.[153] Few letters mention reasons for enlistment, but it is significant that all include fond memories of Bible classes, volunteer bands and Sunday Schools indicating Cornwall's strong connection between religiosity and voluntary enlistment.

The church mostly perceived the war as a holy one, an opportunity to undertake the 'social reconstruction of the nation'.[154] The Bishop of Truro's sermon on 23 August talked of 'licentiousness, lustfulness, gambling, recklessness and drunkenness' and inferred that the war was God's punishment.[155] There were few pacifist Methodist ministers in Cornwall at this time.[156] The views of one Bodmin vicar in September 1914 were clear:

> We are at war with Germany to uphold the neutrality of Belgium ... We are therefore upholding a righteous cause, and we can fight with all our might with a clean conscience ... Let every man whose age and health permits it, think seriously about offering himself as a soldier in defence of his country.[157]

In October the same vicar published Newbolt's address to England,[158] and in December a letter from the War Office[159] appealing for more recruits. Prominent locals also contributed to the campaign, with luminaries such as Hocking[160] and Quiller-Couch outspoken in their support, and active during public meetings. Shirkers were singled out via the pulpit, press and public meetings and women were urged 'kiss no man that can go and won't go' for 'whatever may have been thought of a soldier in the past, today there is not a young woman in all England who is not proud to be seen walking by the side of a soldier in uniform'.[161]

While many recruits' diaries focus on events, those who recorded their reasons for enlistment provide valuable insight into the motivations of volunteers. Most are handwritten and contemporary, clearly not meant for publication. One wanted to 'travel and see the world'. He had no desire to kill Germans but believed it was 'the cause, the honour and glory that leads me on'. He recalled just prior to an attack *The Charge of the Light Brigade* that he had learned at school.[162] Another preferred to volunteer rather than be conscripted, if only because one 'had some choice of unit'. When he heard a Pioneer Battalion of Cornish China Clay workers was being formed, he had asked to join that.[163] One wrote that he 'joined ... to defend our homeland'.[164] Another felt 'the desire to behave heroically is inborn ... in most of us'.[165] One diarist wrote of her brother, 'a man of peace ... he had volunteered because this was a war to end all wars and would make the world safe'.[166]

Other diaries were clearly written retrospectively and meant for publication. They tend to use more emotive language, telling of heroism and patriotism, possibly embellishing the facts for a public readership rather than private reflection, suggesting perhaps that patriotism may have served as justification for less heroic reasons. One such diarist writes of his battalion as 'gallant sons of Cornwall who left home and all they held dear to fight for King and Country, to honour Britain's signature on a scrap of paper' claiming they would 'fight the good fight ... deliver the land of their birth from the devilry of the Hun, to teach him that ... the honour of England ... would ever shine steadfast in the world'.[167]

CONCLUSION

By studying Cornish archives rich in contemporary material including school logs, newspapers, parish magazines, letters and diaries, this article has demonstrated that while the British Empire and militarism were ever present in Cornish life as a result of education, literature and recreation, it was not all-pervasive; Methodism was found to be much more influential in moulding Cornish attitudes and encouraging a deep moral Christian code of conduct which succeeded in inspiring men to enlist once the church was seen to condone the war. The Cornish response to the declaration of war has been analysed to conclude that the Cornish preferred to enlist in the Navy over the Army, reinforcing the county's sea-faring traditions, negative perception of the Army, and perhaps persistent sense of difference to the rest of the country. Once the true nature of the war became apparent and the church advocated support, however, Cornishmen enlisted in the Army because it was the Christian thing to do, showing powerful sentiments of allegiance to their workmates, religious groups and communities. Although Cornwall stands accused of indifference during the early months, newspapers and parish magazines attest to the myriad ways in which the county did rally to provide significant support from all levels of society, towns, villages and communities. Reasons were found to explain why some areas were initially misperceived as having been reticent, making a credible case in Cornwall's defence. This article concludes with a quotation from a volunteer's diary. As the battalion passed another DCLI battalion in the Suez Canal, the men 'gave those lads a good old West Country cheer, and our band struck up *Trelawney*' for 'Cornishmen are clannish, be their meeting place the Land of Pasties, Pilchards, and Cream or the Waters of the Suez Canal', a fitting testament to the Cornish motto[168]: 'One and All' perhaps illustrating the strong sense of kinship the Cornish felt for each other over any powerful sentiments of national or imperial loyalty.

NOTES AND REFERENCES

[1] In memory of George Conium, DCLI, born 1896, killed in action March 1918, aged 21, and his niece, Irene Birch, born 12 November 1920, the day after the unveiling of the Tomb of the Unknown Warrior, named Irene, meaning 'PEACE'. George Conium was born 1896 at St Ann's Chapel, Callington. He was part of the 1/5th battalion of the DCLI. He was killed in action March 1918 during the German Spring Offensive, Operation Michael. His name appears on the Albaston war memorial and on the Pozières war memorial. The 1/5th pioneer battalion's efforts at the counter attack on Verlaines on 23 March were deemed so gallant, they were mentioned in despatches. George was the uncle of Irene Birch, mother of Melanie James. Melanie visited Verlaines and the surrounding battlefields in March 2018, marking the centenary of her great uncle's death.

[2] See for example revisionist theories such as Peter Simkins, *Kitchener's Army, the raising of the new armies 1914-16,* Manchester University Press, Manchester, 1988, Gary Sheffield, *Forgotten Victory,* Headline, London, 2002, Adrian Gregory, *The Last Great War, British Society and the First World War,* Cambridge University Press, Cambridge, 2008, and Catriona Pennell, *A Kingdom United, Popular Responses to the Outbreak of the First World War in Britain and Ireland,* Oxford University Press, Oxford, 2012.

[3] See Stuart Dalley, 'The Response in Cornwall to the Outbreak of the First World War' in Philip Payton (ed.), *Cornish Studies, Eleven,* University of Exeter Press, Exeter, 2003, pp. 85-109, and Pennell, *Kingdom,* p. 149.

[4] Archibald Payton Thornton, 'Review. John MacKenzie, Propaganda and Empire, The Manipulation of British Public Opinion, 1880-1960', Manchester University Press, Manchester, 1984, *The English Historical Review,* Vol. 102, No. 404, July 1987, pp. 752-753.

[5] London Dockers and match-girl strikes of the late 1880s for example. See Stephen Heathorn, *For Home, Country and Race, Constructing Gender, Class and Englishness in the Elementary School, 1880-1914,* University of Toronto Press, London, 2000, and David Silbey, *The British Working Class and Enthusiasm for War, 1914-1916,* Frank Cass, London, 2005, p. 16. China clay strikes in Cornwall in 1913 were brutally suppressed, see Pennell, *Kingdom,* p. 151, and the volume of newspaper cuttings, 1914-1915, DCLI Museum, Bodmin, B1706.

[6] Matthew Hendley, '"Help us to secure a strong, healthy, prosperous and peaceful Britain": The Social Arguments of the Campaign for Compulsory Military Service in Britain, 1899-1914', *Canadian Journal of History,* Vol. 30, No. 2, August

1995, pp. 261-288, p. 263; Jan Rüger, 'Nation, Empire and Navy: Identity Politics in the United Kingdom, 1887-1914', *Past & Present,* No. 185, Nov 2004, pp. 159-187, p. 160.

[7] It was a major shock to the established international order when Japan, a young nation which had copied military development from both old and new empires won the Russo-Japanese War of 1904-1905. See Patrick Porter, 'Military Orientalism? British Observers of the Japanese Way of War, 1904-1910', *War & Society,* Vol. 26, No. 1, May 2007, pp. 1-25; Rüger, 'Nation, Empire and Navy', p. 160. Rüger states that Joseph Chamberlain (British politician and statesman, 1836-1914) coined the phrase of the 'weary titan staggering under the vast orb of its fate' at the colonial conference in 1902.

[8] The belief that the fittest social groups would survive and prevail over weaker groups; Such as J. R. Seeley, *Expansion of England,* MacMillan & Co, London, 1883.

[9] Richard Price, 'One Big Thing: Britain, its Empire, and their Imperial Culture', *Journal of British Studies,* Vol. 45, July 2006, pp. 602-627, p. 616.

[10] John MacKenzie, *Propaganda and Empire, The Manipulation of British Public Opinion, 1880-1960,* Manchester University Press, Manchester, 1984, p. 253; Stephen Heathorn, '"For Home, Country and Race": The Gendered Ideals of Citizenship in English Elementary and Evening Continuation Schools, 1885-1914', *Journal of the Canadian Historical Association,* Vol. 7, No. 1, 1996, pp. 105-124, p. 112

[11] Stephen Heathorn, '"Let us remember that we, too, are English": Constructions of Citizenship and National Identity in English Elementary School Reading Books, 1880-1914', *Victorian Studies,* Vol. 38, No. 3, Spring 1995, pp. 395-427, p. 398.

[12] Heathorn, *For Home, Country and Race.*

[13] Stephanie Barczewski, *Myth and National Identity in Nineteenth-Century Britain, The Legends of King Arthur and Robin Hood,* Oxford University Press, Oxford, 2000, p. 7; Peter Yeandle, 'Empire, Englishness and Elementary School History Education, c.1880-1914', *International Journal of Historical Learning, Teaching and Research*, Vol. 3, No. 1 January 2003, p. 5.

[14] A reference to Sir Henry Newbolt's poem *Vitaï Lampada,* written in 1892 which encouraged selfless commitment and was an inspiration to many during the First World War; From c1870. See MacKenzie, *Propaganda,* p. 2.

[15] See Bernard Porter, The *Absent-Minded Imperialists: Empire, Society, and Culture in Britain*, Oxford University Press, Oxford, 2004.

[16] See David Cannadine, *Ornamentalism: How the British Saw Their Empire,* Allen Lane, The Penguin Press, London, 2001, p. 10. Cannadine's italics.

[17] Porter, *Absent-Minded Imperialists*, p. 38.

[18] Graham Brian Dickason, *Cornish Immigrants to South Africa,* A. A. Balkema, Cape Town, 1978, p. 11.

[19] 44.8% left for overseas with a further 29.7% leaving for other counties from where they were also later to emigrate and be thought of as having originated. See Philip Payton, *The Making of Modern Cornwall: historical experience and the persistence of 'difference'*, Dyllansow Truran, Redruth, 1992, p. 108 and A. Guthrie, *Cornwall in the Age of Steam,* Tabb House, Cornwall, 1994, Dickason, *Cornish Immigrants,* R. Woods, *The Population of Britain in the Nineteenth Century,* Macmillan Education Ltd, Hong Kong, 1992, and D. Baines, *Migration in a mature economy, Emigration and Internal Migration in England and Wales, 1861-1900,* Cambridge University Press, Bath, 1985. This is important in terms of enlistment figures later as many emigrants originally from Cornwall were registered as enlisting at their place of settlement not place of origin.

[20] For example, the Wesley Sunday School in Falmouth received letters and donations for its centenary in 1905 from Canada, Australia, South Africa and Malta, all attesting to fond memories of bible classes and gatherings, CRO MR/F/381. Similarly, diaries include address lists of friends and relations in South Africa and the USA.

[21] Alfred Leslie Rowse, *Autobiography of a Cornishman, A Cornish Childhood,* Jonathan Cape, London, 1942, p. 35.

[22] *Royal Cornwall Gazette* and *West Briton,* January-December 1914.

[23] Silbey, *British Working Class,* p. 53.

[24] Launceston Primary School log book, 1876-1960, CRO SLAUS.

[25] From c1870. See Rüger, 'Nation, Empire and Navy', p. 160.

[26] A succession of displays, culminating in the mock battles and extravagant illuminations at Spithead for the coronation of Edward VII in 1902, demonstrated to the nation and to her allies and enemies, via newspapers and newsreels, her naval superiority. See Rüger, 'Nation, Empire and Navy', p. 165.

[27] Rüger, 'Nation, Empire and Navy', p. 162.

[28] See Dalley, 'Response in Cornwall', p. 87.

[29] See volume of newspaper cuttings, 1914-1915, B1706, DCLI Museum, Bodmin.

[30] Sir Arthur Quiller-Couch, *Nicky-Nan Reservist,* Dent, London, 1929 [1915]), p. v-vi. Quiller-Couch wrote *Nicky-Nan Reservist* in 1915 in defence of Cornwall's war contribution; Ibid, p. v-vi.

[31] See Payton, *Modern Cornwall.*

[32] Silbey, *British Working Class,* p. 67.

[33] N. Ferguson, *The Pity of War,* Penguin Books, London, 1999, p. 201.

[34] Thus read Mrs Ernest Eames in 1899 epitomising the period's ideal of imperialist motherhood and education. Mrs Ernest Eames, *An ABC for Baby Patriots,* Old House Books, Moretonhampstead, 1899.

[35] In 1899, 32.9% of recruits medically inspected were rejected as unfit and described as 'boys and weeds'. See Hendley, 'Help us', p. 266; Anna Davin, 'Imperialism and Motherhood', *History Workshop,* No. 5, Spring, 1978, pp. 9-65, p. 12.

[36] Heathorn, *For Home, Country and Race.*

[37] Davin, 'Imperialism', p. 53.

[38] Yeandle, 'Empire, Englishness', p. 4.

[39] Sir Arthur Quiller-Couch, *Memories and opinions, an unfinished autobiography,* Cambridge University Press, Cambridge, 1944, p. 14.

[40] Brown states that it was the glamorous representation of war which lay behind the reluctance of the toy soldier manufacturer to produce anything other than red-coated figures, even after 1902 when the British Army abandoned its red coats in favour of khaki service dress. Kenneth D. Brown, 'Modelling for War? Toy Soldiers in Late Victorian and Edwardian Britain', *Journal of Social History,* Vol. 24, No. 2, Winter 1990, pp. 237-254, p. 247.

[41] Stephen Humphries, *Hooligans or Rebels? An Oral History of Working-Class Childhood and Youth 1889-1939*, Basil Blackwell Publisher Limited, Oxford, 1981, p. 31.

[42] Heathorn, 'Gendered Ideals', p. 106.

[43] Heathorn, 'Let us remember', p. 398; Pamela Horn, *Education in Rural England 1800-1914,* St. Martin's Press, New York, 1978, p. 252.

[44] Horn, *Rural England*, p. 252.

[45] Gail S. Clark, 'Imperial Stereotypes: G. A. Henty and The Boys' Own Empire', *Journal of Popular Culture,* Vol. 18, No. 4, Spring 1985, pp. 43-51, p. 45.

[46] MacKenzie, *Propaganda,* p. 56; *The New Century Geography Readers Book, Book IVA, The British Isles and Glimpses of Greater Britain,* Blackie and Son Limited, London, 1901, p. 171.

[47] Heathorn, 'Gendered Ideals', p. 123.

[48] Harrowbarrow and Metherell, 1879-1976, CRO LIB/770.

[49] Ibid.

[50] Rowse, *Cornish Childhood*, p. 173.

[51] The Diaries of Miss Agatha Cooke, 1901-1979, CRO X575/1. Her diary also included a newspaper cutting entitled 'Peace at last,' announcing the end of the Boer War.

[52] Recorded by the Falmouth school managers. David Mudd, *The Cornish Edwardians,* Bossiney Books, Bodmin, 1982, p. 65.

[53] Heathorn, 'Gendered Ideals', p. 116.

[54] County Council's Association, Rural Syllabus, 1907, CRO SRC/DC/1/57.

[55] Calstock Continuation School Log, 1876-1903. CRO SR/CALS/3/1.

[56] John Northam of Pencalenick, 12 January 1883, CRO X480.

[57] Launceston Community Primary School log book, 1880-1887, CRO SLAUS.

[58] April 1893, Calstock and Delaware Primary School log book, 1876-1960, CRO SCALS3/1.

[59] Founded in 1877. Located in Tavistock, Devon, just across the border. Kelly College took boarders from Cornwall who travelled by train. Kelly, an independent boarding school reputed for its focus on sports, holds volumes of its

magazine from 1888; *The Kelly College Chronicle*, January 1891 and September 1892. Others include: Woolwich Letter (May 1890), Cambridge Letter (July 1895), Our German Letter (October 1889), India: An Elephant Kraal in Ceylon (May 1913).

[60] Ibid, January 1889 and May 1913.

[61] County Council's Association, Rural Syllabus, 1907, CRO SRC/DC/1/57.

[62] County Council's Association, Rural Syllabus, 1907, CRO SRC/DC/1/57.

[63] Rowse, *Cornish Childhood*, p. 118.

[64] Magazines of Liskeard Grammar School, 1913-1976, CRO AD1546/6.

[65] *The Kelly College Chronicle*, January 1890.

[66] Ibid, May 1913.

[67] Ibid, February 1894, May 1898, July 1898, January 1900 and September 1914.

[68] Ibid, January 1899.

[69] For Bible Christian Methodists in North Devon. The College took boarders, aged 12-16 from Cornwall who travelled by train; Meaning 'To glory through thorns'. No named author, *A School Apart, A History of Shebbear College,* Biddles Ltd, Guildford, undated, p. 8.

[70] Ibid, p. 50.

[71] Ibid, p. 14, p. xv. 130 ex-pupils served in the war.

[72] Founded in 1847 to teach children the importance and principles of temperance.

[73] Patrick A. Dunae, 'Boys' Literature and the Idea of Empire, 1870-1914', *Victorian Studies,* Vol. 24, No. 1, Autumn 1980, pp. 105-121, p. 114.

[74] Susan S. Tamke, 'Hymns: A Neglected Source for the Study of Victorian Culture', *Journal of Popular Culture,* Vol. 9, No. 3, Winter 1975, pp. 702-709.

[75] Callum Brown, *Religion and Society in Twentieth-Century Britain,* Pearson Education Limited, Harlow, 2006, p. 55.

[76] Paul Wilkinson, 'English Youth Movements, 1908-30', *Journal of Contemporary History,* Vol. 4, No. 2, April 1969, pp. 3-23, p. 23; Mark Freeman, 'Muscular Quakerism? The Society of Friends and Youth Organisations in Britain, c.1900-1950', *English Historical Review,* Vol. CXXV, No. 514, May 2010, pp. 642-69.

[77] Brown, *Religion and Society*, p. 46; Bernard Deacon, *Liskeard and its people,* Bernard Deacon, Redruth,1989, p. 65.

[78] Rowse, *Cornish Childhood,* pp. 128-29.

[79] Eddie Collins, *No Red Coat For Me, Miles of Memories,* (transcribed oral history, 1993, Duke of Cornwall's Light Infantry Museum, Bodmin, Cornwall), p. 14; Oral history entry in Harrowbarrow and Metherell School Log, 1879-1976, CRO LIB/770.

[80] Payton, *Modern Cornwall,* p. 90; Quiller-Couch, *Nicky-Nan,* p. 35.

[81] The Cornwall Record Office shows considerable Band of Hope activity in Cornwall after 1877. For example, in 1885 Liskeard alone had 14 Bands of Hope with a total of 1,034 members. All but two of these Bands of Hope were

connected to Methodist Sunday schools, further reinforcing the links between religion and temperance. See Adrian R. Bailey, David C. Harvey, Catherine Brace, 'Disciplining Youthful Methodist Bodies in Nineteenth-Century Cornwall', *Annals of the Association of American Geographers,* Vol. 97, No. 1, March 2007, pp. 142-157, p. 153.

[81] Brown, *Religion and Society*, pp. 59-75.

[82] Begun in the 1850s with 400 children, rising to 900 in the 1870s. See Deacon, *Liskeard and its people,* p. 91.

[83] See Deacon, *Liskeard and its people,* p. 68.

[84] The Boy Scouts Association Local Association Returns; Falmouth Scout Rally, June 1910, 200 boy scouts from Falmouth and Penryn attended, see *1st Camborne (Roskear) Scout Group, Cornish Scouting and Social History,* Edited by Colin French, Institute of Cornish Studies, Sources of Cornish History, Volume Two, Penwell Ltd, Callington, 1993, p. xiv.

[85] Collins, *No Red Coat,* p. 14.

[86] Parish Magazine of St. John the Evangelist, Truro, January 1906, 1896-1911, CRO P 238/2/227.

[87] Such as one to Marconi's wireless telegraphic station. See Parish Magazine of St. John the Evangelist, Truro, July 1906, 1896-1911, CRO P 238/2/227; Parish Magazine of St. John the Evangelist, Truro, September 1911, 1896-1911, CRO P 238/2/227.

[88] One describes a choirman's visit to Devonport Dockyard to see HMS Lion. See Bodmin Parish Magazine, September 1910, CRO P13/2/260.

[89] See Bodmin Parish Magazine, September 1910, CRO P13/2/260.

[90] Another reference to Newbolt's *Vitaï Lampada* which illustrates how the public school ethos filtered down to the working classes. Parish Magazine of St. John the Evangelist, December 1896, Truro, 1896-1911, CRO P238/2/227; Bodmin Parish Magazine, April 1913, CRO P13/2/260.

[91] Bodmin Parish Magazine, September 1911, CRO P13/2/260.

[92] CRO MRCA/217.

[93] MacKenzie, *Propaganda*, p. 214; For an example, see Latchley Parish Magazine, 1879, Calstock Parish Archives, Gunnislake, Cornwall.

[94] MacKenzie, *Propaganda,* p. 18.

[95] Rowse, *Cornish Childhood,* p. 117.

[96] George Alfred Henty, 1832-1902.

[97] Such as The Tiger of Mysore (1896) and With Kitchener to the Soudan (1903).

[98] L. R. N. Ashley, *George Alfred Henty and the Victorian Mind,* International Scholars Publications, Bethesda, 1998, p. 334.

[99] Ferguson, *Pity,* p. 1.

[100] MacKenzie, *Propaganda,* p. 204.

[101] Ibid, p. 205.

[102] See Jeffrey Richards, 'Spreading the Gospel of Self-Help: G.A. Henty and Samuel Smiles', *Journal of Popular Culture,* Vol. 16, No. 2, Fall 1982, pp. 52-65.

[103] Tehidy Working Men's Club, 1913-1933, CRO X857.

[104] See Deacon, *Liskeard and its people,* p. 85.

[105] Redruth Literary and Debating Society Syllabus 1897-1899, CRO X481/24.

[106] Bodmin Parish Magazine, June 1914, CRO P13/2/260; *Royal Cornwall Gazette,* 5 March 1914.

[107] See A. Michael Matin, 'The Creativity of War Planners: Armed Forces Professionals and the Pre-1914 British Invasion-Scare Genre', *ELH,* Vol. 78, No. 4, Winter 2011, pp. 801-831, p. 811; MacKenzie, *Propaganda,* p. 40.

[108] See The Advertising Archives, www.advertisingarchives.co.uk, and Melanie James, *Why was there so little effective opposition to the war in Britain between 1914-1918?,* April 2013.

[109] *Royal Cornwall Gazette,* January-June 1914.

[110] Ibid.

[111] Rowse, *Cornish Childhood,* p. 196.

[112] *Royal Cornwall Gazette,* 2 July 1914.

[113] *Royal Cornwall Gazette* and *West Briton,* July 1914.

[114] *Royal Cornwall Gazette,* 28 July 1914.

[115] *West Briton,* 1 August 1914.

[116] *Royal Cornwall Gazette,* 6 August 1914.

[117] Ibid.

[118] Ibid.

[119] Quiller-Couch, *Nicky-Nan,* p. vi.

[120] *Royal Cornwall Gazette,* 20 August 1914.

[121] *West Briton,* 6 August 1914; Ibid, 27 August 1914, p. 2.

[122] *Royal Cornwall Gazette* and *West Briton,* August-December 1914.

[123] For example, John Sturge-Stephens was training for the Church and was on a German exchange when war broke out. He was a member of the Falmouth Peace Association and campaigned ardently for peace even when a young boy at school. On the outbreak of war, he helped refugees and offered his services to support the nation in any capacity other than killing but was arrested. See correspondence of John Sturge Stephens, 1903-1914, CRO ST341/1 and Papers of Pacifist Movement 1898-1916, CRO ST301. Bernard Walke, well known Anglican pacifist of St. Hilary from 1912, tried to bring all denominations together for the restoration of peace, in an association he called the Brethren of the Common Table but his meetings were broken up and he was misunderstood and suspected, see H. Miles Brown, *A Century for* Cornwall, The Diocese of Truro, 1877-1977, Oscar Blackford, Truro, 1976, p. 74.

[124] See Guthrie, *Cornwall,* Dickason, *Cornish Immigrants,* Woods, *Population* and Baines, *Migration.*

[125] Volume of newspaper cuttings, 1914-1915, DCLI Museum, Bodmin, B1706.

[126] Ibid.

[127] *West Briton,* 7 September 1914.

[128] Quiller-Couch, *Nicky-Nan,* p. v-vi.

[129] The Navy did not send the information in time prior to publication.

[130] Winifred Hawkey for example refers to her cousin who emigrated to Australia and fought at Gallipoli, see Winifred Hawkey, *Memoirs of a Redruth Childhood,* Dyllansow Truran, Redruth, 1987, p. 110.

[131] Quiller-Couch, *Nicky-Nan,* p. v-vi.

[132] Review of the *Royal Cornwall Gazette* and *West Briton,* January-June 1914.

[133] Bodmin Parish Magazine, December 1914, CRO P13/2/260.

[134] Diary of Private H. M. Kendall, DCLI Museum, Bodmin, D6021.

[135] Bernard Walke, *Twenty Years at St. Hilary,* Methuen, London, 1936, pp. 61-64.

[136] Volume of newspaper cuttings, 1914-1915, DCLI Museum, Bodmin, B1706.

[137] In the *West Briton,* 6 August 1914, one farmer remarked that the commandeering of horses would hinder harvesting operations to a considerable extent; Volume of newspaper cuttings, 1914-1915, DCLI Museum, Bodmin, B1706.

[138] Brown, *A Century for Cornwall,* p. 73.

[139] Volume of newspaper cuttings, 1914-1915, DCLI Museum, Bodmin, B1706. The following year, newspapers talk of the 'recruiting boom in the clay area' when 230 miners were recruited in two weeks.

[140] *West Briton,* 27 August 1914.

[141] Volume of newspaper cuttings, 1914-1915, DCLI Museum, Bodmin, B1706.

[142] For example The Diary of Miss Elsie Stephens, 1914-1916. 'Charlie was longing to enlist in some way – he had been declined on account of his health.' CRO ST 201.

[143] One individual shouted "Let them fight who have something to fight for" and another said "I ain't going to enlist, I don't trouble what happens." Volume of newspaper cuttings, 1914-1915, DCLI Museum, Bodmin, B1706.

[144] Elizabeth Hotten, *Cornwall at war, memories, letters and reflections from the parish magazines,* The History Press, Stroud, 2008, p. 29.

[145] Review of the *Royal Cornwall Gazette* and *West Briton,* August-December 1914.

[146] See the volume of newspaper cuttings, 1914-1915, DCLI Museum, Bodmin, B1706, and *The Liskeardian,* December 1914, CRO AD1546/6.

[147] The National Archives, Kew: CAB 37/122/164, Recruiting in proportion to population, 12 November 1914.

[148] See John Charles Cripps Probert, 'Recruiting for the 1914-1918 War and the Religious Census', *Journal of the Cornish Methodist Historical Association,* Vol. 9, 2000, pp. 130-135, p. 131.

[149] Ibid, Probert, p. 135.

[150] See volume of newspaper cuttings, 1914-1915, DCLI Museum, Bodmin, B1706.

[151] The letter was signed 'A Callingtonian, 26 April 1915.' See volume of newspaper cuttings, 1914-1915, DCLI Museum, Bodmin, B1706.

[152] Quiller-Couch, *Nicky-Nan,* p. vi.

[153] Correspondence of John Sturge Stephens, 1903-1914, CRO ST341/1, and set of volunteer letters, MRR/1003; Via soldiers on leave but also via their letters published in newspapers, e.g. 'Letters from the front' in the *Royal Cornwall Gazette,* 24 September 1914. Sapper McKenny of Redruth tells of his role in the Battle of Mons and 'revolting German treatment'.

[154] Ted Bogacz, '"A Tyranny of Words": Language, Poetry, and Antimodernism in England in the First World War', *The Journal of Modern History,* Vol. 58, No. 3, September 1986, pp. 643-668, p. 660; Gregory, *The Last Great War,* p. 160.

[155] *West Briton,* 23 August 1914, p. 2.

[156] Brown, *A Century for Cornwall,* p. 73.

[157] Bodmin Parish Magazine, September 1914, CRO P13/2/260.

[158] Bodmin Parish Magazine, October 1914, CRO P13/2/260.

[159] Bodmin Parish Magazine, December 1914, CRO P13/2/260.

[160] Respected Cornish author, heavily involved in recruitment, 'wheeled in ... as one ... who could paint an attractive and heroic picture of life at the front,' his novels providing moral justification for those who felt uneasy in the light of Christian teaching. See Alan M. Kent, *Pulp Methodism, The lives and literature of Silas, Joseph & Salome Hocking, Three Cornish Novelists,* Cornish Hillside Publications, St Austell, 2002, p. 170.

[161] Volume of newspaper cuttings, 1914-1915, DCLI Museum, Bodmin, B1706.

[162] Diary entry of Walter Harris (Private Bogey), DCLI Museum, D9690.

[163] Diary of John Henry Drew, 10th Battalion, DCLI, DCLI Museum, Bodmin, John is referring to his father.

[164] Ibid.

[165] Diary of Private H. M. Kendall, DCLI Museum, Bodmin, D6021.

[166] Elizabeth Flawn, *The Saga of a Cornish Family, 1882-1975,* Utd Writers, Cornwall, 1995, p. 83.

[167] Reminiscences of a Territorial in the DCLI on Service in Europe, Asia and Africa in The Great War, p. 10, DCLI Museum, Bodmin, D11541.

[168] Ibid.

'I HAVE NOW HAD A LOOK AT THE LAND OF "COUSIN JACKS" AND PASTIES: CORNISH AUSTRALIANS IN CORNWALL DURING THE GREAT WAR

Philip Payton

INTRODUCTION

In 1927, in an article on Cornish emigration in Cornwall County Council's celebratory *Cornwall Education Week Handbook*, edited by Q (Arthur Quiller Couch), Harry Pascoe mused on the enduring links between Cornwall and Australia. Almost a decade since the end of hostilities, he looked back nostalgically to the sometimes bitter-sweet atmosphere of those days, recalling the Great War years 'when scores of Australian khaki clad soldiers sought out remote corners of the County to visit for the first and last time the homes of their fathers'.[1] For Australians on the Western Front, there was little hope of returning home half-a-world away while hostilities lasted, unless they were one of the lucky few to be granted an extended furlough or were repatriated as invalids no longer fit for service. In such circumstances, Britain – 'Blighty' – assumed great significance as a home-from-home. Many Australians had been born in the British Isles, and even those for whom Australia was the land of their birth, Britain remained the 'old country', an enduring focus of loyalty and affection. Moreover, many Australians had relations in various parts of the United Kingdom, and leave periods, or recuperation from wounds, or postings to British training camps, were eagerly sought opportunities to visit kith and kin and renew perhaps fading family links. Returning to the bosom of an extended family in Britain, a reprieve from the horrors of the trenches, was, in its way, almost as good as going home.[2]

Not surprisingly, given the scale of the nineteenth-century mass emigration from Cornwall, there were numerous Australians of Cornish descent serving on the Western Front during the Great War years, and, as Harry Pascoe observed, not a few visited the 'remote corners' of Cornwall, many 'for the first and last time'. There were those, as Pascoe noted regretfully, who were never given the opportunity to make a return journey, some because they had lost their lives in battle before they had a chance to do so, others because they had been repatriated quickly at the war's end. In this brief article, we investigate the experiences of a small sample of those Australian soldiers who did make their way to the Cornwall of their parents or grandparents. None, for various reasons, ever returned again, as we shall see.

EDGAR RULE AND *JACKA'S MOB*

Among those who wished to nurture family links was Edgar Rule, born in1886 in the outback copper-mining town of Cobar in New South Wales. Brought up a Methodist, he was keenly aware of his Cornish descent, and, as part of his attempt to rekindle family ties, embarked on an intimate correspondence with his (unnamed) Aunt in Cornwall, visiting her when sent on a training course on Salisbury Plain in early 1918. In lengthy, no doubt cathartic, letters, Edgar Rule provided his Aunt with an unparalleled series of insights into life in the trenches. Consciousness of his Cornish roots he may have been, but he shared in the Australians' emerging sense of national identity, as he made plain in his correspondence.

Returning from his training course in Wiltshire, Rule rejoined his unit at Allonville, near Amiens, at the end of April 1918, having just missed the Australians' resolute defence against the German spring offensive, including their decisive recapture of Villers-Bretonneux on Anzac Day (25 April). 'Well, I've got back to the battalion and right glad I am, too', he wrote to his Aunt in Cornwall: 'We came here about midday after a nine mile march . . . we came in contact with numbers of French soldiers, and a very fine lot they were'. He thought their brass band poor – 'the worst balanced band I've ever heard: it seemed to be composed mostly of French horns, trumpets, and lots of small instruments' – but enjoyed the camaraderie:

> It is remarkable how all the French people look up to our fellows, in spite of their 'kick ups' [antics]. Several times, as a couple of us walked by, French women would say: 'Australia beaucoup swank!'. As soon as our boys showed up here in the old billets that we occupied during the Somme fight in 1916, the Frenchies said: 'It's all right, Australia here!'. To-night I took a picket into a neighbouring town to look after any who might have imbibed too freely, and I ran against an old French couple with two bonny little girls. The little girls and I chummed up, and the old people invited me in to have a cup of coffee, and it was amusing to notice the respect they seemed to have for Aussies. One little girl was very much like Edna used to be.[3]

Edgar Rule's Aunt may have enjoyed the insights into French provincial life, but she must have been extremely broad-minded to have appreciated her nephew's description of the aftermath of the battle of Villers-Bretonneux. The Australian troops, Rule explained, scoured the abandoned houses for treats or souvenirs, although much had already been looted by the Germans during their brief occupation. 'Cupboards lay wide open', he wrote, 'and, though most of the eatables had gone, we could still have picked up quite a lot of tapioca, coffee, chicory, and such stuff, and potatoes galore'. Moreover:

> In their bedrooms everything had been pulled down on the floor. Beautiful underwear belonging to the women lay all around, and had been trampled on by each visitor; yet there was quite a lot still clean. My boys were very dirty and chatty [lousy], and before we had passed the third house the beggars had changed their old dirty stuff for beautiful chemises with pretty pink ribbons; some had even changed their underpants for garments never made for men. One humourist had on a big silk bell-topper. Ladies' nighties were quite the fashion, and one of the boys lined up next morning for his breakfast arrayed in a beauty.[4]

Rule also provided his Aunt with glimpses of what it was like to be in the midst of battle, such as his description of his participation in the Australian victory at Hamel on 4 July 1918. As they advanced towards the retreating Germans, he said, 'one of our own shells burst about ten yards away, and down went my batman, Dave Floyd, in a heap just alongside me. He lay there, looking at us quite calmly, realizing that we could not attend to him, and I think he knew he was fatally hit'. Then, a few yards further on, 'Stan Cochrane, one of my corporals, received a bullet through the head which must have killed him instantly though none of us saw him fall, and he lay hidden in the wheat crop'. As Rule's platoon moved closer to the enemy, 'I saw a fellow's head come up and take a look at me. Bang, and down he went. Whether I hit him or not I don't know, but I found a Hun lying there afterwards'. Subsequently:

> The rest of them scooted off up a trench, and as we got to our objective we found two dugouts . . . When I yelled out to the occupants, out came two hands with a loaf of black bread in each, and presently a pair of terrified eyes took a glimpse at me. They must have been reassured by my look, because the Huns came out at once, and, when I sized them up, all thoughts of revenge vanished. We could not kill children, and these looked to be barley [sic] that. If any of us had been asked how old they were, most of us would have said between fourteen and fifteen.[5]

'This about all the news just now', he signed off nonchalantly. 'Don't be too excited about our victories', he added, noting that the swift outcome at Hamel was the result of detailed planning and the careful co-ordination of all-arms warfare (aircraft, tanks, artillery, infantry): 'Our staff work today is such that victory is almost a foregone conclusion before we go over the parapet'.[6] As Rule anticipated, it was only a matter of time before the Germans collapsed on the Western Front. Thereafter, he remained in contact with his Aunt but, for reasons unknown, never revisited Cornwall, being repatriated to Australia during 1919. However, Edgar Rule's letters to his Aunt were saved for posterity, and they were incorporated into his later book *Jacka's Mob*, first published in 1933, a history of the 14th Battalion, named after the unit's hero, Albert Jacka, himself of Cornish stock, who had been awarded the Victoria Cross at Gallipoli. As the Moonta *People's Weekly* had reported proudly at the time: 'The first VC to come to Australia was won by . . . [a] Cornishman in the person of Lance-Corporal Jacka'.[7]

'WE WERE AUSTRALIANS OF CORNISH DESCENT'

The interest shown at Moonta, in the heart of the 'Little Cornwall' copper-mining district of northern Yorke Peninsula in South Australia, in Jacka's exploits, indicated that, alongside Imperial loyalties and a nascent Australian nationalism, regional distinctiveness was also important. It was no surprise, then, when Australian soldiers from Moonta, and the adjoining townships of Kadina and Wallaroo, made their way to Cornwall as soon as they were able. When Lloyd Pollard had first arrived in Britain in 1916, part of a contingent of new recruits fresh from Australia, bound for the training camps of Salisbury Plain, he had written excitedly to his parents at Moonta Mines, explaining that he had landed at Devonport and 'could see a piece of Cornwall just over the River Tamar, which divides Cornwall from Devonshire'. Moreover, the 'first thing I had to eat was three good pasties, on the wharf – boys selling them for 3d. each'. [8]

After an initial period of training (he was a private in the 11th Field Ambulance), Lloyd Pollard was granted leave, and headed straight for Cornwall. 'At last I can write to you about my trip through dear old Cornwall', he later wrote to his parents, 'the places you used to speak of when Roy and I were boys . . . we used to hear dad and grandfather speak of the places I had the pleasure to see'. Pollard enthused about conducting 'my first conversation with a Cornishman in his native country . . . It was grand to hear the Cornish dialect'.[9] But all too soon leave expired, and at last he was posted to France. There, alas, he met with a serious accident. Some heard that he had been injured while assisting in the construction of a field hospital.[10] Others thought that he had damaged his back while bringing in the wounded under fire at Armentieres and that, 'it being the second coldest winter in France for nearly 50 years, it affected his spine so much that he never recovered'.[11] An X-ray and medical examination diagnosed 'caries of the spine', attributed to 'exposure and infection', and Pollard was evacuated to England for treatment. At the hospital in Epsom, his doctors reported that he suffered severe pain in the 'lumber region of the back on slightest movement'.[12] Little could be done for him, and he was duly repatriated to Australia. Confined to bed for over two years, Lloyd

Pollard died in the military hospital in Keswick, Adelaide, on 14 April 1919.

Lloyd Pollard's never-to-be-repeated visit to Cornwall was a fleeting one as it had been so much anticipated. Equally fleeting was the visit of Bert Grummet, who managed to fit in a trip to Cornwall after a spell in hospital at Stratford-upon-Avon (where he had soaked up the district's literary and historical associations). Grummet's forebears hailed from the Harz mountains of Germany (another copper-mining region) but he was considered as good a Moonta boy as any other, not least because his father had published *The Christmas Welcome: A Choice Collection of Cornish Carols* at Moonta in 1893.[13] At any rate, Grummet made the almost obligatory pilgrimage to Cornwall, reporting on a postcard to the Moonta *People's Weekly* that 'I am enjoying furlough in lovely Cornwall'. He had admired Stratford, he said, 'which is also is lovely, but it is a different kind of beauty to Cornwall'.[14]

More substantial was the Cornish sojourn of Private Leigh Treweek Lennell, a Moonta boy who had been seriously wounded in the battle of Lone Pine during the Gallipoli campaign. Evacuated at first to Malta (his right arm having been amputated at sea) and then to England, he found himself at the Fulham Military Hospital, where he was to have an artificial arm fitted.[15] 'I am in excellent health', he wrote reassuringly to his mother, 'and my arm has healed up splendidly'. It was certainly 'hard luck losing my arm, especially the right' but most of his mates had been killed at Lone Pine, and 'one has to be thankful if he gets out of this war alive'. Besides, people in Britain had been extraordinarily generous, and 'we are having the time of our lives. It is indeed a change after the Dardanelles'. The 'people simply idolise our boys and take us for motor rides all over the country'. In this way, he said, he had 'visited many beauty spots, and have been to some wealthy people's places for tea'.[16]

Moreover, Leigh Lennell had had a 'stroke of good luck', as he put it, as at the hospital he had bumped into 'a Kadina boy I know really well. His name is Art Trenwith', a former Wallaroo miner from Moonta Road in south Kadina. Lennell had also met Art Trenwith coincidently at Gallipoli, and now in London they had again been reunited by fate: 'It was just like being home again to meet someone I knew so well'.[17] Some weeks later, writing to his mother, he explained that he was now in a nursing home at Putney, where 'I am well cared for, and am having a jolly time . . . [at] times I think it is worth losing a limb for . . . they can't do enough for me'. He had had an artificial arm fitted, but it was 'not much use'. He also announced that 'I expect to spend a week in Cornwall shortly with the Matron of this home, Miss K.M. Cosgrave', adding swiftly that he would be accompanied throughout: 'Art Trenwith is going also'.[18]

Soon Leigh Lennell was writing to his mother from the Tywarnhayle Hotel at Perranporth: 'You will see from this address that I am down with the Cousin Jacks'. He was enthralled, exclaiming that it 'is perfectly lovely here, and just like home again'. As he explained, the 'people talk exactly like the Cornish at Moonta . . . and as soon as the people knew we were Australians of Cornish descent, they crowded around us and talked for hours'. They were 'making us Cousin Jack pasties', he added, and his new-found friends were anxious to take them to places of interest across Cornwall. He listed the localities they had already visited or were soon to see – Redruth, the Lizard, Land's End, Truro, Penzance, Carbis Bay, St Ives, Newquay, Bedruthan Caves, the St Agnes tin mines – 'in fact every place down here'. The sense of affinity with local people was overwhelming. 'I feel sure some of them must have relatives in Moonta', he speculated: 'Such names as Polkinghorne, Pengilly, Polgreen, Penberthy, are all old folk here'. Moreover, their dialect and accent were reassuringly familiar, enhancing the sense of home-from-home: 'They all say, "How art 'e getting on, ma son", and "Es, boy, es" . . . we can understand them all and talk like them'.[19],

A few days later, Leigh Lennell wrote home from the Land's End Hotel. 'While at Penzance a very peculiar thing happened', he confessed: 'We were in a shop buying some south-wester hats and were talking to a young man who said he came from South Australia. When asked what part, he said "Moonta Mines"'. Then unfolded a story, recounted almost incredulously by Lennell, in which a strange intimacy was unveiled, with Leigh Lennell and Art Trenwith immersed in a community half-a-world away from home that was uncannily familiar in its coincidences. As Lennell explained, having exchanged introductions with the young man from Moonta Mines, they were invited to visit 'the shop next door and see his people'.[20] He went on:

> I did, and who do you think they were? Mr and Mrs Rowe and family, who lived just by Truer's shaft and close to Penberthy's. We were all delighted to see each other. I was in the same class as the daughter, Pearl. We had a long talk, and they gave me some 'People's Weeklies'. I also met a Miss Penberthy, related to Moonta folks by the same name. Messrs Rowe and Penberthy are partners in a grocery business. They enquired of all their old Moonta friends . . . I shall be very sorry to leave here.[21]

But, of course, leave they did. Having completed his rehabilitation, Leigh Lennell was repatriated to Australia, where he was discharged from the armed forces. He arrived back at Moonta in early May 1916 to a hero's welcome.[22] In the November he married Violet May Anderson of Broken Hill, a mining town across the New South Wales border with close Moonta connections.[23] Meanwhile, Art Trenwith was returned to the Western Front, joining his unit at Bapaume. On the morning of 17 February 1917, which broke with slight mist and drizzle, he was engaged in bringing up bombs to the front line near Switch Trench in preparation for a raid. Unfortunately, the Germans were active too and, surprised by the enemy, Trenwith was caught off guard and killed. His mother, back in Kadina, was told that her son had been shot cleanly through the head.[24] But others knew otherwise, one soldier explaining that he 'was with me on a party carrying up bombs to the front line at Swiss [*sic*] Trench . . . The Germans started bombing us and he was blown up . . . He was blown up without doubt but I did not see his body'.[25]

'PLAY THE GAME, BOYS, DURING THIS TIME'

More fortunate was the experience of Signaller Lance Corporal Leonard John Harvey. Born at Moonta of Cornish descent, his father was the Hon. William Humphrey Harvey, a former moulder at the Moonta mine workshop and secretary of the Moonta Miners' Association from 1897 to 1915, when he was elected a Labor member of the South Australian Parliament.[26] Leonard Harvey knew both Leigh Lennell and Lloyd Pollard (and was much distressed by the latter's incapacity and eventual demise), such was the tight-knit nature of the community on Moonta Mines, the mineral lease settlement adjoining Moonta township. He had first arrived in Britain in July 1917, having landed at Southampton from Le Havre after a lengthy journey by troop train across France from Marseilles. It was to be the first of three trips to Blighty (as he called it), the second when he was at Burdon Military Hospital in Weymouth (recovering from 'gassing'), and finally in the (northern) spring of 1919 as he awaited repatriation to Australia. During his time at Weymouth, Harvey had planned a visit to Cornwall with his mate Jack Pyatt, another Cornish-Australian from Moonta (who had been badly wounded on the Somme), but before the arrangements could be made, he was posted to Salisbury Plain in preparation for his return to front-line duties in France.

The much-anticipated trip to Cornwall had to be postponed until May 1919, when Leonard Harvey was in Britain, waiting his turn to be repatriated to Australia. Thousands of other Australian soldiers were likewise waiting to go home, and for many it was a boring and frustrating time as the months passed.[27] Shortly after the Armistice in November 1918, General William Birdwood, the officer commanding the Australian Imperial Force, had issued a memorandum to his troops. He foresaw, he said, that 'demobilisation will undoubtedly be difficult and irksome' and that 'great personal restraint will certainly be required'. Australia's name stood high in the Empire, Birdwood emphasised, and it was up to them to ensure that it was not compromised by 'any behaviour of ours'. Ships to take Australians home would inevitably be in short supply, and everyone would have to take their turn. 'Play the game, boys, during this time', Birdwood implored, 'as you have always done, and add still more to the gratitude which will always be acknowledged to you by the Empire and remembered by me as your comrade and commander'.[28]

Many Australians had a soft spot for 'Old Birdie', and Leonard Harvey seemed touched by Birdwood's heartfelt plea for patience. Carefully folding Birdwood's memorandum, and placing it among his own papers, Harvey did indeed 'play the game' during his remaining time in Britain. Most especially, he and Jack Pyatt finally made their trip to Cornwall. As he explained in a letter home to Moonta in April 1919, he and Jack were to spend a few days in London before 'going down to Cornwall, to see a few of "They Cousin Jacks"'.[29] They caught the overnight train from Paddington, arriving at Camborne the next morning, where they were met by Mrs Bennett, Jack's aunt. They stayed almost a fortnight and, as Harvey noted in his diary, they made the most of their time in Cornwall. There was the customary trip to view Land's End, and visits to Penzance (where they met Dick Rowe, the grocer from Moonta), St Just, St Ives, Sennen, Mousehole, and Helston, the latter being prepared for Flora Day on 8 May. They even found time to attend a rugby football match between Cornwall and New Zealand – a 'Win for NZ', as Harvey recorded in his diary.[30] Reflecting on his visit, Leonard Harvey wrote with evident satisfaction to his father: 'So you can see we have had a look at the land of "Cousin Jacks" and Pasties'.[31] On 3 May he was one of the 5,000 Dominion troops that marched through London, and on 20th of that month he embarked at Liverpool in the transport steamer *Nestor*, bound at last for South Australia.

'I COULD DOFF MY HAT IN HONOUR / TO THE MOONTAS NEAR OUR GATE'

Lloyd Harvey and Jack Pyatt were numbered – like Edgar Rule, Lloyd Pollard, Bert Grummett, Leigh Lennell and Art Trenwith – among those 'scores of Australian khaki clad soldiers' who had visited Cornwall during the war years. They were 'six bob a day tourists', comparatively well-paid by British standards, who had the means as well as inclination to visit Cornwall (as well as other far-flung corners of the United Kingdom), helping to bolster the Cornish tourist industry during what otherwise might have been lean years. But they had also sought out relations and places with family associations, on occasions meeting individuals who had returned to Cornwall from Australia years before, and – in the case of Edgar Rule – initiating a lengthy correspondence which helped to ameliorate the worst of life in the trenches. But, as Harry Pascoe had intimated, it was a two-way process, and people in Cornwall were often as moved as their Australian cousins by these renewed contacts and exchanges.

Although none of her letters has survived, we know that Edgar Rule's Aunt wrote often and apparently at length to her nephew, the arrival of the Americans on the Western Front prompting Rule to write: 'In future I want you to put "Australian Imperial Force" on my mail instead of A.I.F. The reason is that the Yanks, who have lately come over, are putting "A.E.F." [American Expeditionary Force] on their mail, and a lot of our mail is being mixed with theirs'.[32] Such was the emotional value of his Aunt's correspondence, that he could not bear for it to go astray. Back in Cornwall, George Jose, a former Moonta miner now residing at Illogan, put pen to paper to celebrate the links between Cornwall and Australia, especially the recent rekindling of contacts and affections. In his poem, 'Moonta and the Great War', he honoured 'the valiant stand of Moonta, / With her few heroic men', and welcomed the soldiers to his home, hoping for a permanence in this rekindling and imagining the joyful union of visiting Australians and local Cornish girls:

I could doff my hat in honour
To the Moontas near our gate,
And I'm proud to pen this tribute –
Moonta's little, but she's great.

Though I'm not an aged prophet,
Though I'm not an honoured seer
I'd predict this – without question,
In the marriage lines so dear –

There'll be many an Australian soldier
Linked with some sweet Cornish girl.
Who could blame them? Not the writer.
He would e'er their flag unfurl.

He would throw the rice and slipper,
And his joy would ne're abate,
And he writes with lasting pleasure –
Moonta's little, but she's great.[33]

As if to concrete the relationship and confirm the sentiment, George Jose's poem found its way to the *People's Weekly* in Moonta, where it was published on 21 August 1921.[34]

NOTES AND REFERENCES

[1] Harry Pascoe, 'Cornishmen and Emigration: The Adventurous Cornish Miner', in Arthur Quiller Couch (ed.), *Cornwall Education Week Handbook*, Cornwall County Council, Truro, 1927, p.145.

[2] Philip Payton, *Regional Australia and the Great War: 'The Boys from Old Kio'*, University of Exeter Press Exeter, 2012, pp.111-138; Philip Payton, *Australia in the Great War*, Robert Hale, London, 2015, pp.141-162.

[3] Edgar Rule, *Jacka's Mob: A Narrative of the Great War by Edgar John Rule*, ed. Carl Johnson and Andrew Barnes, Melbourne Military, Prahan (Vic), 1999, p.115.

[4] Ibid., p119.

[5] Ibid., p.133.

[6] Ibid., p.138.

[7] *People's Weekly*, 14 August 1915.

[8] *People's Weekly,* 16 September 1916.

[9] *People's Weekly*, 6 January 1917.

[10] *People's Weekly*, 18 April 1919.

[11] *People's Weekly*, 26 April 1919.

[12] National Archives of Australia [NAA] B2455/8019308 Lloyd Ewart Pollard.

[13] Philip Payton, *Cornish Carols from Australia*, Dyllansow Truran, Redruth, 1984.

[14] *People's Weekly*, 24 August 1918.

[15] NAA B2455/8298155 Leigh Treweek Lennell.

[16] *People's Weekly*, 20 November 1915.

[17] Ibid..

[18] *People's Weekly*, 15 April 1916.

[19] Ibid..

[20] Ibid..

[21] Ibid..

[22] *People's Weekly*, 13 May 1916, 20 May 1916.

[23] *People's Weekly*, 13 January 1917.

[24] *People's Weekly*, 17 March 1917.

[25] Australian War Memorial [AWM], Australian Red Cross Society Wounded and Missing Inquiry Files, 1914-18 War/ 1DRL/0428 1822 Private Arthur Aubrey Trenwith, 10th Battalion; NAA B2455/8394022 Arthur Aubrey Trenwith.

[26] NAA B2455/8019308 Leonard John Harvey; for an account of the Cornish influence in the South Australian Labor movement, see Philip Payton, *One and All: Labor and the Radical Tradition in South Australia*, Wakefield, Adelaide, 2016.

[27] Philip Payton, *'Repat': A Concise History of Repatriation in Australia*, Department of Veterans' Affairs, Canberra, 2018, pp.19-29.

[28] National Trust of South Australia, Moonta Branch Archives [NTSAMBA], 'In the Best of Health and Spirits': The Letters and Diaries of Signaller Lance Corporal Leonard John Harvey, unpub. manuscript compiled by Rob and Carol Howard, Elizabeth M. Scott, Diana Kay Arula, and John Campbell Harvey;

Memorandum: General Bridwood, 'In the Field, 14 November 1918', To the Officers, Non-Commissioned Officers and Men of the Australian Imperial Force.

[29] NTSAMBA, Letters and Diaries, Letter, 9 April 1919.

[30] Ibid., Diary entry, 26 April 1919.

[31] Ibid., Letter, 2 May 1919.

[32] Rule, *Jacka's Mob*, p.117.

[33] Philip Payton, *Making Moonta: The Invention of 'Australia's Little Cornwall'*, University of Exeter Press, Exeter, 2007, pp.167-168.

[34] *People's Weekly*, 21 August 1921.

FROM *MEETING THE KAISER* TO *AN TANKOW*: IMAGINING THE FIRST WORLD WAR IN CORNISH AND ANGLO-CORNISH LITERATURE AND THEATRE[1]

Alan M. Kent

INTRODUCTION: CULTURE AND CONSTITUENTS

Perhaps the most noticeable physical reminder of the impact of the First World War on Cornish communities was the post-war flourishing in memorial architecture: principally Celtic-knotwork and Celtic cross-inspired monuments to the fallen,[2] but also Breton-style lantern crosses,[3] and other markers of the Cornish involved in or killed in the war.[4] In the aftermath of the conflict, certainly in these kinds of visual testaments to those lost, in contradiction to its growing and enforced Anglicisation, Cornwall seemed to re-engage with its Celtic past on a hitherto unexpected scale. This re-engagement was not fully isolated, however, from other movements in Cornwall.

Since the late nineteenth century, a revival of interest in Cornwall's ancient Celticity had taken place, which saw antiquarians and scholars looking to the past to find a way forward for Cornwall, both politically and culturally.[5] The fact that the First World War put a temporary hold on those 'internal conflicts' of the constituent parts within the British union in the face of a wider enemy, did not fully negate them or discontinue them.[6] One only has to look at events in Ireland in 1916 to see this.[7] However, even in the memorial Celtic crosses, one notices the paradox of Cornish Celticity versus integration into Britain (or more specifically, England). Although perhaps not as vociferous as say, voices in Ireland, Cornwall too, was starting to contest its position as a complicit constituent part of the union— albeit on an embryonic scale. This was the wider union that was involved in fighting Germany and its allies during the Great War.

The architectural monuments that have survived in Cornwall are a very physical reminder of the brutality of the conflict during the First World War (not to mention the successive conflicts which have followed), and as part of our childhood experiences in the education system, we grow up with an understanding that a very specific kind of literature appeared to have developed out of the context of the First World War. Principally, this takes us to the 'classic' set of war poets (such as Wilfred Owen, Siegfried Sassoon and Rupert Brooke) who documented not only the initial misplaced enthusiasm for the conflict, but also their later disbelief in its four-year long futility.[8] The image of that literature is seared onto the cultural memory of most students (and adults), and it has embedded onto our culture a particular lens through which we see the conflict.[9] Our understanding of the conflict has also been informed by popular culture in a range of works, from Welsh-language film (*Hedd Wyn*) and serious television drama (*The Monocled Mutineer, The Crimson Field*) to 'black' comedy (*Blackadder Goes Forth*).[10] Some other prose and drama texts have assisted in this process. Among the most famous prose texts are Vera Brittain's *Testament of Youth* (1933), Pat Barker's *Regeneration* trilogy (1991-1995) and Sebastian Faulks' *Birdsong* (1993).[11] Drama has offered satire in early works, such as *Night Watches* by Alan Monkhouse (1916) and *Tunnel Trench* by Hubert Griffith (1924), but also classically, in Joan Littlewood's *Oh! What a Lovely War* (1963), and more recently in *The Accrington Pals* by Peter Whelan (1982) and *Sea and Land and Sky* by Abigail Docherty (2010).[12] These works have helped define our responses to the First World War in the wider British context.

Cornish and Anglo-Cornish Literature is perhaps not always readily thought of as having too many links to the First World War, and its imagining in poetry, prose and drama may seem slight compared to say, either the 'cultural nationalist' stylings of literature with the language of Cornish itself, and the often romanticized depiction of Cornish experience, carried through much of Anglo-Cornish literature during the twentieth century, at least.[13] However, although perhaps not as visual or as constant in our memories as the monuments of the fallen—once we examine the continuities and discontinuities of literature developed from Cornwall during the First World War, its immediate aftermath and its long-term impact, we see that, in fact, a specific genre of writing has emerged, which equates to much of the wider literary response to the war, but seen here in microcosm from this Atlantic ocean 'periphery'. Overall, it would appear that certainly at the opening of hostilities, Cornwall as a whole, was not enthusiastic at entering a new war, but due to 'imperialist' pressure from its closest neighbour, as the war persisted, young men and women from Cornwall reluctantly volunteered. There may even have been latent feelings over earlier foreign wars, such as the Crimean War (1853-1856) and the more recent Boer War (1880-1881), a conflict with a lasting impact on the Cornish working in South Africa.[14] As a number of observers have commented, it was probably the legacy of Cornish Methodism that encouraged people to do the right thing and join up.[15]

It is my intention in this chapter to offer a survey and an introductory consideration of the way in which Cornish and Anglo-Cornish literature has imagined and constructed a particular vision of its response to the First World War. In so doing, we will undoubtedly consider the paradigms of identity and cultural memory. Such a response is often contained in sometimes 'hidden' literature, though one has to note that in the twenty-first century, in particular, there has been a very active and sustained theatrical response to the war: a genre which may, to a certain extent, not come as unexpected, seeing as how Cornwall's main literary tradition has, over the centuries, been mainly dramatic.[16] Perhaps curiously, there has overall, been less of a poetic response to the War: a fact that has to be considered in the light of the overwhelming development of verse from other writers outside of Cornwall. In this sense, an individual Cornish response may have seemed unnecessary, given the weight of the poetry already developed. For example, in the two major collections of Anglo-Cornish poetry that have emerged recently, there are few responses to the First World War;[17] the same may be said of the equivalent volumes for poetry in Cornish.[18] Maybe too, there was an unconscious or psychological pressure to adopt an English and then a wider British frame of reference.

Three important points also need to be made about the contemporary literature developed during the conflict, and that which was shaped in its immediate aftermath, as compared to that which has followed in successive decades. Literary studies never seek 'the truth' in the sense that it never can, but it may well be the case that the later literature has been shaped by a particular lens through which the First World War has been seen, and that we should be sceptical and careful about how that lens may have distorted the real historical events. Secondly, likewise, we need to consider the contemporary literature carefully, for it may well have needed time to 'settle' and really understand the intricacies of the war. Thirdly, we also must be sceptical of applying a 'reading' informed by our own biased and pre-constructed visions of the war.

A related point is that writing this article as I am, in the second decade of the twenty-first century, it is clear that we are now in a phase where the last veterans of the conflict (through natural death) are no longer able to supply the researcher with oral accounts of their experiences. Indeed, much was made by world media of the death of one of the last surviving veterans of the conflict—Harry Patch.[19] It is certainly the case in viewing some of the more recent imaginings of the war, that there has sometimes been a romanticization of the conflict (however much unintended), observed in texts such as Michael Morpurgo's famous children's novel *War Horse*,[20] later adapted into a play, where seemingly the armoured industrial twentieth-century (tanks, heavy artillery, mustard gas, armoured shipping) are still working in union with a pre-industrial form of warfare (horses, cavalry, men lining up to face each other in hand-to-hand conflict, the old order of the British army). Indeed, it would seem that this collision of cultures stands as one of the most shocking elements of the First World War: that suddenly this was killing and death on an industrial scale. For an industrial territory such as Cornwall, this transition—already experienced in mining and engineering—was reinforced even further.

Because of these factors it is no longer critically good enough to view the literature related to the First World War as simply a 'catalogue of human disaster', The historical context for both the contemporary literature of the war itself, and that which emerged in its aftermath, and that of more recent origin, needs substantial locating of the implications of these texts in history. When we do this, we are free to consider in Christopher Hampton's important term, 'the ideology of the text',[21] and locate the literature in its specific economic, political, religious and social context, so that the modes and mechanisms of production and reception of that literature are more readily understood. This critical framework, which I have been suggesting for a number of years now,[22] allows us to more realistically assess the significances of different literary texts over time. It also negates a 'liberal humanist' response to Cornish Studies, and facilitates fresh investigation, not blinkered by either micro-studies of the past, or Anglo-centric distorted assessments of Cornish experience.[23] This reading is political. It also embraces aspects of popular literary culture ignored by outmoded and old-fashioned literary studies.

When examining the literature imagining the First World War, it is worth bearing in mind that throughout the twentieth century, studies of the conflict have tended to examine the wider British 'unionist' experience within the war,[24] and have focused less on the individual component nations and contested territories within the United Kingdom. This would seem to match the utilitarian need to 'pull together' to combat a greater foe, and negate internal tensions and divisions, as well as those individual nations' and territories' sometimes distinctive response to the war. Even some studies of the twenty-first century have continued this agenda of invented 'Britishness'.[25]

However, of late, this position has changed substantially and more historians and scholars are beginning to tease out those separate and distinctive responses.[26] In addition, there are emergent studies of how migrant communities from other parts of the globe, played their part in the conflict; for example, Payton's recent study of the importance of the migrant Cornish to the Australian war effort, and Mathai and Kendall Hall's examination of the Indian contribution to the British war effort.[27] Broadly then, studies on the First World War are shifting from their classic narrative into more considered responses. Not only has this process occurred, but there have also been shifts of late to consider the conflict beyond the depiction of the trenches, to other areas of the war,[28] and to the significance, for example, say, of the under-representation of naval battles in the North Sea.[29] Also noticeable are a growing set of publications which examine the wider implications of the war within alternative groups and on a global scale (outside of western Europe).[30] These studies have often emerged in tandem with events marking the centenary of the beginning of the conflict, such as the art installation of the cascade of porcelain poppies (designed by Paul Cummins and Tom Piper) completed at the Tower of London in 2014, and in 2016 the 'shrouds of the Somme' event in Exeter.[31] It is in such public art where we can partially locate contemporary Cornish responses to the war.

New Cornish Studies has perhaps been guilty in the past of not necessarily giving the First World War due attention. However, the reasons for this are somewhat obvious. Scholarship has tended to consider other aspects of Cornish experience concurrent with the war; including the Celtic Revival, political and economic changes affecting Cornwall's relationship with its nearest neighbour (England), wider literary studies, emigration, the growth of tourism, and industrial decline. The narrative of the war is generally seen as punctuating this wider sense of Cornish experience during this phase. Indeed, it may be, that as this volume notes, the Cornish response to the First World War is a suitable area of treatment.

Articles so far in *Cornish Studies* have been thin; the exception being Stuart Dalley's 2013 examination of the response in Cornwall to the outbreak of the First World War.[32] In wider scholarship, some initial work has been completed: for example, Pete London's *Cornwall in the First World War* (2013) and Nick Thornicroft's *Cornwall's Fallen: The Road to the Somme* (2008).[33] Both of these works are populist in intent; the latter being heavily illustrated with photographs. Some related publications have also emerged. Among these are, for example, Cassandra Phillips' editing of the diaries of Marjorie Williams during the war years, and occasionally studies, diaries and letters from the period are published in Cornish-related books, magazines and journals.[34] Diaries and letters sometimes shift curiously into the realms of literary study, and given that there are so many in existence, it may not be possible in an article of this length to cover the full range of texts.

However, some works are more relevant; in particular perhaps because the observations of Cornish women during the conflict are more likely to be found there. Their silence in all genres of literature is noticeable. We do know the reasons for this (a patriarchal and sexist publishing system, general limitations placed on their achievement and limited opportunities in education), but sometimes we have to admit defeat when trying to trace sources and publications.[35] Within the investigation, it is also perhaps useful to pick through some of the most famous 'literary' autobiographies documenting this period, for they too, offer us insights and paradigms on how the conflict was both perceived and 'constructed' in Cornwall, and how the war informed their later writing.

THE CORNISH LITERARY CONTEXT OF THE FIRST WORLD WAR

In the nineteenth century, like most territories across Western Europe, Cornwall had witnessed the rapid growth of the novel. Novels tend to develop in places experiencing rapid transition from traditional agrarian lifestyles into industrialization, and Cornwall stands symbolic (and perhaps too, an innovator) of this process.[36] Visiting and indigenous novelists had seen the potential of imaging the 'world of Cornwall' both in romanticized and realist ways.[37] This process had continued on into the early years of the twentieth century, although we might argue that the First World War marks a moment in the ultimate conclusion of this industrialization project. The war and its effects put a juddering stop to this manner of operation, where lead characters in novels were always in conflict with the society around them.

The halt was caused because here was a war which actually shifted the narrative perspective. Now characters in novels faced a modern Europe in conflict on an industrial scale. For the Cornish, side-lined by the wider Celtic movement, as being 'too English' and not 'Celtic enough', whereas in actual fact, the group are more readily defined as being 'industrial Celts' (somewhat more practical, less agrarian and 'in tune with nature'). This conceptualization of the Cornish in this way, however, is helpful to our understanding of how they were perceived in fiction. The wider result was that the motivation and context of the novel needed rethinking and re-aligning. Realism rose to the surface: it had to, considering the level of death being experienced. However, that was not to say that romanticism disappeared entirely. In times of conflict, often readers seek romanticism to take them away from the horrors of the contemporary. We might therefore note a cultural shift in terms of reader response: the novel was altering hand-in-hand with the demands of wider European Modernism.[38] Indeed Modernism itself may be seen as one response to the First World War. In the aftermath of the war, established conventions were swept away. In particular, the Great War led to further secularization of British society, initially brought upon by reflection on Darwinism, but then later by a question over a Christian God who could seemingly allow such destruction to happen. The novel may also have stalled slightly in terms of its wider production and development. Despite the rise in literacy at the end of the nineteenth century, novels and fiction were being consumed in new ways. Serialization of the novel declined. Fiction tended to be purchased in a single volume format. The result of this was the novels did not have the length that they had in previous decades. In this sense, they became more portable. Although the rise in mass media (via radio and television) was really a few decades off, publishers were noting shifts in public tastes and had to cater for them.

There is, indeed, an argument that this period may well be the point at which the short story finds its own audience,[39] and that short stories allowed readerships to cope with the wider transitions: to, in a sense, allow the novel to 'settle' again. Hence, although we note a wider growth in the short story genre during the war years and its immediate aftermath, this was not the case for Cornwall. Indeed, the short story genre—like the female voice—is noticeably absent. This would appear strange since often the short story, being a genre in which experimentation with form and subject-matter can take place, may well have been a suitable one in which writers might test the water with War stories. This appears not to have been the case though.

Cornwall had already started to be romanticized in the second half of the nineteenth century. Not only were folklorists at work in documenting this peripheral Celtic territory that was rapidly industrializing,[40] but also industrialization itself was coming to be romanticized (a trajectory, that moving forward, would have an even greater effect in the post-Second World War period).[41] Therefore, in some senses, an overall pattern can be determined where the romanticism and tranquillity of Cornwall are contrasted heavily with the horrors of the Front. Not only did this reinforce Cornwall's physical distance from the war, but also furthered its place of 'untouched' Britishness (a contradiction in itself), since there were those already pushing for Cornish (and thus 'ancient Briton') self-control. There may even be noted a rise in historical romanticism, where readerships simply wanted escape from reality—and this is borne out in the number of texts which, say, feature traditional motifs of Cornish experience: adventure fiction about smuggling, piracy, shipwrecks and romantic love upon the cliff-tops. As we shall see though, Arthurian matter was not pillaged in this way.

In most usual accounts of literary activity in Britain, drama is seen as going through an unproductive phase during the late nineteenth century, and that compared to the novel, plays went through a crisis of their genre which left the British stage bereft of quality drama. The usual notion was that they were non-literary and populist. This view has been revised of late, noting the actual popularity of theatre during the period, and new views of certain writers and texts have emerged.[42] That same scrutiny has now been given to drama in Cornwall during this period and many undiscovered and previously unconsidered texts have had light shone upon them.[43]

The period during the First World War has a similar picture, where drama about Cornwall did emerge, though perhaps one has to look a little more carefully to locate it. Certainly, like the novel, romanticization upon the stage was highly sought after—to sweep audiences away from what was occurring in the war—and there were few contemporary, realist dramas emerging out of Cornwall during this phase. It may be that people had no desire to see such work, or that dramatists had not found ways of depicting the conflict. As mentioned above, only a few contemporary wider British dramas emerge in this period, so it was perhaps likely that Cornwall might develop its own individualized response. On the other hand, the move may be seen as breaking the continuum of writing from Cornwall, which, as I have demonstrated previously, has always led the way with constructions of place and people from a theatrical point of view. There might, for example, have been a response to the war that could have come through the tradition of mystery play writing in Cornwall, but this would have to physically wait until the 1940s (and the Second World War) with texts such as *Bewnans Alysaryn [The Life of St Alysaryn]* by Peggy Pollard (1941).[44] Again, one wonders if the shock of the conflict almost impeded writing. That said, Pollard's work was a cynical inter-war response to secularization and failing Christianity—some twenty-five years after the First World War. One might therefore even argue for a latent literature emerging.

However, there are other factors in place in the case of drama written in Cornish. No new writing of this mystery play format had emerged in the eighteenth or nineteenth century and (bar a few shorts skits in revived Cornish) it would only be at the end of the twentieth and beginning of the twenty-first centuries that the genre would develop again. Likewise, none of the dramatists or poets yet had the skill to offer such a response. If we do consider this a central part of the Cornish literary continuum, then such a theatrical literary response was only seen in the dramatic work of Charles Causley (who is resoundingly an Anglo-Cornish writer of the Second rather than the First World War).[45] In fact, a glance at the advertisements for dramatic productions in the Cornish newspapers of the period show not only a shut-down in the range of shows occurring,[46] but also a remarkable lack of plays which contemporize or depict the war in realist ways. As mentioned above, this might be because public tastes did not warrant it, or it may also be for practical purposes. Young men were away at conflict.

There were decreased audiences and probably a lack of money to see theatre. It may well be culturally the backbone of Cornish literature but during this phase, the Cornish seemed to distance themselves from the genre that had defined them. Maybe it was regarded as just too frivolous or inconsequential. This view would seemingly match the wider British response to the war and to theatre.

With regard to the Second World War, as mentioned above, Charles Causley may be regarded as a poet who seems to encapsulate experience of the conflict— both at home and in his time in the navy.[47] There are other poets too, who have depicted this phase of Cornish life in reaction to the 1939-1945 conflict.[48] When we look at the First World War however, there are few poetic figures depicting the conflict. The response is either found in obscure journals or magazines or comes in the constructions of experiences of poets from later in the century or imagined by those interpreting historical events at a later date.

The same break in the continuum as with drama may be noted here then, although if one trawls enough sources it is present, and there may be deemed a hidden poetic response to the wider war. Often, this is infused with Christian ideology, and of a kind of 'wider crusade against evil'—a position that in Methodist Cornwall emerged once cynicism over a wider 'English war' dissipated. Specific moments in the war are rarely marked. This may be because writers did not always receive the instant media of the current world and events and shifts in the war came through to the public more slowly. There was maybe even a sense that government propaganda was covering up some of the atrocities experienced which might have resulted in poetic responses (as seen in say later response to modern 'media' wars in say, Vietnam, Northern Ireland and Iraq). Victorian poets had never been averse to dealing with contemporary evils (here one immediately thinks of Alfred Lord Tennyson's *The Charge of the Light Brigade*[49]) but there certainly appears to be a slow response to depict the 1914-18 war in poetic terms in Cornwall.

If we consider poetry in Revived Cornish then this was very much in its infancy around this phase, so it is hardly surprising that little material emerges (perhaps though, with one exception, as we shall see below). Poets in Cornish were barely able to begin their first steps in reinvigorating the language, let alone deal with the complexities of the conflict around them. That said, however, as their writing did grow it tended to look at iconic visions of 'Cornishness' (often romanticized and medievalized), and certainly influenced by the continuum of Breton as a language, instead of what Kennedy has recently termed 'useful culture'.[50] This article certainly allows us to ponder the question as to what might have happened, if some of the early Revivalist poets and writers had engaged more fluidly with the First World War. Would the subject matter have been more relevant—and therefore would Cornish people have looked upon the Revival with different eyes? This is perhaps wishful thinking to some. The Revival was what it was—and did what it thought it needed to do—in order to make the language and culture stand on its own two feet again. However, as we shall see, some different responses may be noted, and these are interesting to locate within the wider academic debate over the Cornish Revival and its ideology.

It is perhaps only in the distant aftermath of the conflict that novelists, dramatists and poets have truly come to terms with events that took place. Distance and time are sometimes required by writers in order to begin to process the immensity of the conflict that has occurred. Here again, the twin notions of Realism and Romanticism come into play. Sometimes the distance can perceptively alter the realism with which a particular event is dealt with. It some ways, it can be romanticized but it can also be given a kind of 'hyper-realism' which was not in place at the time. Realism can also remind audiences and readers of the tragedy of the situation, and that they are left helpless, in the sense that they can do nothing to change events of the past. However, anti-war literature can also inspire present generations to ensure that they follow more pacifist and diplomatic solutions to external conflicts. We are led to believe that we can with the right solution or can promote positive change. Literature therefore assists in this process. Romanticism though, can be a dual-edged sword. The very fact that the First World War has been romanticized has assisted the way in which culture has dealt with it. The way it is interpreted generally leads again to a pacifist response to culture.

However, as we fully know from the historical romantic tradition in Anglo-Cornish literature, it can also distort reality. Therefore, contemporary writers and readers have a tricky path to negotiate. The response to the First World War, its initiation and its aftermath are also now being re-read once again in the context of post-'Brexit', where Britain and Cornwall are renegotiating their relationship with the wider European Union. This understanding of the historical and contemporary trends within Anglo-Cornish, Cornish and Cornu-English writing should help us to appreciate the literature that has emerged from this relatively small European territory in response to the First World War. Given the auspicious nature of the conflict, this is unlikely to end in the near future, and this collection of essays is a timely response: a marker in the sand, if you like, of our current assessment of literary production arising from the conflict. Revised interpretations are to be expected from readings of this survey and are a desirable part of the critical reassessment being made.

IMAGINING THE WESTERN FRONT AND NAVY THROUGH CORNISH EYES: THE NOVELISTS

The leading contemporary novelist of the First World War was the St Stephen-in-Brannel-born novelist Joseph Hocking (1860-1937). As I have extensively detailed,[51] Hocking came from a writing family; his older brother Silas Kitto Hocking was the first British novelist to sell a million copies of one novel,[52] and his younger sister Salome Hocking has good claim to be the first working-class female Anglo-Cornish novelist.[53] Like his brother Silas, Joseph Hocking entered the Methodist ministry but soon began to realise, like his brother, that his 'moralistic fiction' could actually do much good, and so he stepped away from the pulpit to become a novelist. This was so his literary preaching could travel further and be received and heard by more people.

Joseph Hocking was, like Silas, incredibly successful as a writer, producing almost one hundred novels that became the staple reading diet, not only of a growing literate and Methodist population in Cornwall, but also in wider Britain and Ireland,[54] and to wherever the Cornish travelled to across the globe.[55] Hocking's fiction has three distinctive phases: the first of which was generally historical and anti-Catholic. He may even, as I have suggested elsewhere, have good claim to be the founder of the historical romantic novel within Cornwall.[56] With these texts, his fiction was often set between the fifteenth and seventeenth centuries, and assumed a highly Protestant position. In many ways, this matched the development of the novel, which might in some quarters, be considered a 'Protestant' literary form.[57] Put another way, it is the form of literature that has developed anew in the post-Medieval period.

However, with the rise of the First World War, Hocking's fiction shifted, and he began to document and construct fictional imaginings of the conflict which were highly successful—if sometimes a little fantastical. They very much considered the Great War, however, from a Cornish point of view, and with Cornish characters often placed in the midst of the conflict. In this way, Hocking was able to take his readership to various locations around the European and Middle Eastern theatres of war. The conflict, however, produced a notable change in his ideology.[58] Hocking began to realise that the greater evil was not so much Catholicism but, in fact, the rise of Germany. He discovered that many Catholic countries and cultures were engaged in this wider and more important fight, and so his position as an ultra-Protestant activist shifted markedly. We note in both his correspondence and fiction a transition to be more sympathetic to Catholicism.

During the First World War, Hocking was active as a recruiting force within Cornwall. His religious position, and status as a preacher and novelist, made him a minor celebrity who travelled to various Cornish towns and villages to encourage young men to sign up. Hocking was not always successful in his endeavour, but he was persistent. The Cornish were cynical about joining up. No doubt, these experiences informed the construction of his fiction. As demonstrated below, Joseph Hocking would later be re-imagined as a character in the Anglo-Cornish twenty-first century play *Surfing Tommies*.[59]

The final phase of Joseph Hocking's writing intersects with the wider Celtic Revival in the post-World War One period. Joseph's softening of his response to Catholicism allowed him to look more closely at the Celto-Catholic heritage of Cornwall, with a particular fascination for saints and their lives. He also embraced an antiquarian interest in ancient monuments, and, in so doing, his fiction altered to pioneer the connections between the present and the past—a form of writing that was to influence the construction of texts such as initially, Arthur Quiller Couch and later, Daphne du Maurier's co-write of *Castle Dor*.[60] During this phase, Hocking left behind his need to develop reflective writing about the war. Seemingly, once the conflict was over, there appeared to be less purpose in continuing to write about it. Maybe Hocking felt it was best put to bed.

I now turn to offer a more detailed consideration of Hocking's wartime texts. It is clear that Joseph Hocking's fictional examination of the First World War forms a considerable thematic concern in the developing of his writing. Joseph was aged fifty- four when hostilities were declared, already having shaped many successful novels. So far, both his historicised vision of Protestantism and fictional fight against Catholicism had formed the basis of his work. This was now about to change. Joseph saw his fiction of the conflict as 'literary weapons' designed to support the cause. It was in his view, a holy war. As Appleby perceptively notes, Joseph 'saw his production of novels as a positive contribution to the struggle against Germany, and they were clearly written to provide moral justification for active participation in hostilities, especially among those who would have felt uneasy in the light of Christian teaching, and to encourage recruiting'.[61] It was a position that diverged considerably from that of Silas, whose son Arthur died during the aftermath of the war in 1919. Having put so much energy into the war effort, and having seen his son survive the War, his death came as a bitter blow, and probably contributed to Silas's swift decline in health.[62]

A few contextual and thematic observations are helpful. Initially the novels were written to match contemporary events, but texts like *The Kaiser's Investments* continued to deal with the aftermath of the War as late as 1920.[63] Most often, Joseph's war heroes were of Cornish extraction, from middle-class mining families, who are offered commissions on the nod, but who often choose to join the rest of the 'Tommies' in the thick of the action.[64] The novels detail the conditions in the trenches, as well as broader issues surrounding the conflict, often culminating in a spell in a segregation or prisoner-of-war camp.

Joseph often integrates his usual technique however, whereby the characters come, by fate and circumstance to meet 'real' figures; for example in *All For a Scrap of Paper: A Romance of the Great War* (1915), the protagonist, Bob Nancarrow gains a face-to-face interview with the Kaiser after being captured by the Germans.[65] This is an interesting fusion as it demonstrates the 'hyper-realism' that Joseph was seeking within his writing. His aim was to make the 'romance' as relevant as possible by integrating real figures whose historical narrative had yet to be fully determined. By using such characters as Nancarrow, Cornish heroes were placed in the 'thick of the action', and so the fictionalisation of the war became more relevant to readers. The technique also embodies a sense of purposefully representing popular opinion about Germany that was felt both in Cornwall and across wider Britain. Crucially, novels like *The Curtain of Fire* (1916) and *The Pomp of Yesterday* (1918) express the vast scale of the conflict, as well as the human cost.[66] Despite this, it has to be observed that Joseph was not moved in the way other, now more famous writers and poets of the period were.[67] Blind patriotism is the overwhelming concern.

The core novel of the period is *Tommy: A War Story* (1916), which has a different construct from outset.[68] The 'Tommy' hero is a young man from a working-class background in Lancashire (though constructed in such a way as it could be industrial Cornwall), who goes on to have a distinguished battle career and on the way, exposes a spy. Joseph was also keen to make sure his military writing was accurate. As a disclaimer in *The Pomp of Yesterday*, he notes in his foreword:

> Neither are the descriptions of the Battle of the Somme the result of the writer's imagination, but transcripts from the experiences of some who passed through it. Added to this, I have, since writing the story, paid a second visit to the front during which I transversed the country on which Thiepval, Goomecourt, La Boisselle, Contalmaison and a score of other towns and villages once stood. Because of this, while doubtless a military authority could point out technical errors in any description, I have been able to visualise the scenes of battle and correct such mistakes as I made at the time of writing.[69]

Joseph drew on much real experience in such novels. He had travelled widely within Europe, so knew the landscape and settings of the Western Front, as well as those in the Middle East. He had also been heavily involved with the recruitment campaigns of the early part of the War, visiting a training camp on the Sussex Downs in 1915. In this, he seems to have been 'wheeled in' as one of those respected figures who could paint an attractive and heroic picture of life at the front, even at one point coming back to Cornwall when the War Office felt they were not making the desired impact there. In an interview in the *Daily Chronicle* quoted in the *Cornish Guardian*, Joseph claims this was how his task was described to him:

> The Cornish are a very clannish people and are suspicious of strangers. But you are a Cornishman. You know the people and they know you. You are acquainted with their history, their characteristics, their language. They have not done well as far as recruiting is concerned; won't you go and arouse their Celtic fire?[70]

Considering that the Cornish Revival was broadly operating at the same time as this, such a position is paradoxical. 'Celtic fire' was not necessarily appreciated in terms of internal difference in wider Britain, but was desired in terms of military aggression for the conflict. The 'clan' ideal was also important to note, for it suggested a solidarity and their 'suspicion of strangers' would seem helpful in wartime. Ironically too, these markers also set them apart and demonstrated Cornish difference. In the midst of this cultural confusion, Joseph was trying, in modern terms, to put 'positive spin' on what the Cornish were and could be in times of war. As well as this, Joseph took a hard-line with 'shirkers', showing wherever possible in his fictions either the results of not enlisting, or the glory that could be obtained. Joseph's hope was that Cornishmen would be as persuaded by his rhetoric as they were in John Wesley's day, but after addressing meetings elsewhere in Britain, he found the Cornwall he had returned to was very different than the one he had left, commenting that 'the people instead of being easy to move are adamant. Young men laugh at appeals to the emotions, flights of oratory leave them cold... They are not stolid; they are stony. They will listen keenly, intelligently, critically and show no sign'.[71] Maybe at this point, for the Cornish, the war was an 'English' one that had little connection to Cornwall. Were the Cornish happy enough to continue in their traditional industries of mining, farming and fishing? It would seem so. A further noteworthy point is that although numbers for recruitment to the army appeared low, there is strong evidence that many Cornishmen chose (following almost instinctual maritime behaviour) and signed up for the Navy (another reason perhaps for Cornish absence in wider accounts). This frustration, however, is given a different spin in *All for a Scrap of Paper*:

> Events have moved so rapidly in our little town of St Ia, that it is difficult to set

them down with the clearness they deserve. We Cornish people are an imaginative race, just as all people of Celtic origins are, but we never dreamed of what has taken place. One week we were sitting idly in our boats in the bay, the next our lads had heard the call of their country, and had hurried away in its defence. One day we were at peace with the world, the next we were at war with one of the greatest fighting nations in the world.[72]

Here, the 'Celtic fire' is further embedded by a construct of the Cornish being 'an imaginative race'. The implication here again juxtaposes two images of the Cornish. The imaginative idea seems on the one hand to suggest that such an ethnic group is wistful and full of story and narrative (not necessarily the best skills for military service) but on the other hand, this could also refer to Cornish engineering and invention (a perhaps prouder tradition of 'industrial Celticity' than 'imagined' storytelling). Hocking, and other recruiters like him, were trying to find ways to appeal deep into the heart of the Cornish. The 'Celtic fire' option perhaps did not work well enough because for the past thousand years, the English had been effective in trying very hard to extinguish and dampen down any Cornish 'Celtic fire'. Nevertheless, despite his concern that not enough young Cornishmen were enlisting, Joseph maintained his stance throughout the conflict. Appleby, following Thorne, makes a useful summary of the ideological, not to mention propagandist, themes of the novels:

1. The Germans are a good people misled by the Kaiser who is sincere but mad.
2. Germany was responsible for the war. It was not a war she had drifted into because of her alliances but the war had been planned by her in advance.
3. It was a religious war because the rulers of Germany were under the influence of such writers as Trieshke and Neitzsche who advocated a philosophy that might was right.
4. Britain was riddled with German spies, most of whom spoke good English and could display impeccable loyalty to this country to the extent that they could even join the armed forces of this nation and play a double role. Their names could be Anglicised.[73]

This list makes for interesting reading—expressing as it does the very practical problems that caused the conflict. We note not only here the responsibility of Germany for the war (though one has to assert that the actual historical events which began the conflict are complex and contested) but Hocking seems to have recognised a philosophical basis for their mistaken behaviour. Point 4 seems somewhat more 'propagandist' and maybe even a little 'wild' in terms of accuracy. Such a view makes for paranoia, of the kind that was experienced by the novelist and poet D. H. Lawrence and his German wife Frieda, when in 1917-18 she was supposedly signalling to German submarines whilst living at Zennor in

West Cornwall.[74] Despite the madness of this accusation, such paranoia may well have been ignited by just the kind of propaganda that Hocking and others were writing. Lawrence re-imagines these events in his 1923 novel *Kangaroo*, in a chapter titled 'Nightmare'.[75]

These attitudes at home in Cornwall were reinforced by a deliberate imagining of British heroism in the conflict. In *All for a Scrap of Paper*, the novel's epilogue is an imaginary letter, with Joseph attesting the virtues of joining up:

> When I have time to write properly, I shall have some wonderful things to tell you concerning the heroism of our army... If only we had more men, we could put them to rout and that right quickly. That is our great need. More men like the London Scottish who have simply covered themselves with glory... You should hear what the men at the front are saying about the shirkers who are hanging back. They are a disgrace to the country and deserve to be flogged... If ever God called volunteers to fight in a Holy War, it is now.[76]

Here the agenda is double-edged. It seems that the Celtic origins of the London Scottish are heroic enough already, while the Cornish Celts are sadly lacking in the same kind of bravery. The implication too, is that some of the shirkers are the Cornish who had not yet enlisted. The seeming focus on 'our great need' suggests a purely English agenda of involvement, where the constituent parts of the union are conveniently ignored. It seems that here Joseph had been sold on this construct. However, this was to change in the post-war period. We note that the conflict had long lasting reverberations in Joseph's novels. The naïvety which had accompanied some earlier narratives dropped out, once statistics of the numbers of dead started to reach Britain. When the reality of this hit the British public, Joseph's jingoism became decidedly low key.[77]

In the post-war period he had to reinvent himself again. This reinvention took several paths. Joseph's attacks on Roman Catholicism lessened after the War, when Britain drew on support from many Roman Catholic countries. It seems that Joseph realised there were more important enemies. His writing returned now to more historical themes, with a gentler pro-Protestant stance. The fiction then returned to explicitly Cornish subject-matter, retreating from the grander European themes, ideologically letting his brother Silas, pick up the pieces. Once the post-war discussion was over, Joseph eased back to write some of his most famous texts: *Andrew Boconnoc's Will: The Story of a Crisis* (1926), *Bevil Granville's Handicap* (1926), *The Tenant of Cromlech Cottage* (1927), *Felicity Treverbyn: A Love Story* (1928), *Nancy Trevanion's Legacy* (1928) and *The Secret of Trescobel* (1931).[78] Many of these novels were set in the present day, with lingering doubts over the conflict of the previous decade, but as noted above, relied on Cornish Celticity for their inspiration and resolution. *The*

Tenant of Cromlech Cottage stands out in this respect, not only with its tongue-twisting protagonist 'Gwithian Trewithen', but because of its association of the Cromlech (or quoit) with Cornwall's Celtic past (misplaced, since most chamber tombs date from much earlier, yet are, as Chapman has observed, intrinsically connected with Celtic peoples[79]). Hocking's portrayal of the First World War was not perfect, but he was a writer in the right place at the right time and managed to encapsulate some of the energy of the period. His eventual retreat into Celticity away from English imperialist ideology conveniently matched the war memorials being built around Cornwall in the 1920s.

More or less contemporary with Joseph Hocking was the novelist, poet and critic Sir Arthur Quiller Couch (1863-1944) who took the literary pseudonym of 'Q'.[80] As John Hurst has noted in his useful assessment of Anglo-Cornish Literature made in 1992, Quiller Couch's importance to the development of literature and literary studies in the late nineteenth and early twentieth century was paramount.[81] Born in Bodmin, but from a family heralding from long-standing connections to Polperro, Quiller Couch went on to become King Edward Professor of English at the University Cambridge, but spent considerable time back in Cornwall—from 1891 onwards—living and working in Fowey.[82]

Many of Quiller Couch's novels featured Cornish themes, and so it was likely —with the advent of the First World War—that a fusion of world events and literature would occur. It is believed that after a reversal of family fortunes (his mother getting into debt), Quiller Couch turned to fiction in order to generate money, and before 1900 he had published over thirty novels, many of which form the 'bedrock' of late-nineteenth-century Anglo-Cornish literature.[83] They are often distinctly Cornish in terms of character and identity, but also work as well-plotted action and adventure tales, possibly in the spirit of other writers such as Robert Louis Stevenson and H. Rider Haggard.[84] Like Hocking, Quiller Couch's novels often depict maritime themes and are set in coastal locations.

The early focus however, tended to be on character. This changed to events and themes with his later fiction, and indeed in one of Quiller Couch's texts which will be our focus here. This was *Nicky-Nan: Reservist*, which was published in 1915.[85] The novel was clearly based on Quiller Couch's own extensive experience of recruiting young men to fight in the war. This was very similar to the context in which Joseph Hocking was writing. A further context should be identified, however. In 1888 Quiller Couch had married his wife Louisa, and they had a son, Bevil, who fought and survived the conflict, but succumbed to pneumonia in 1919—a series of events which very much matched the experiences of Silas Kitto

Hocking.[86] General critical opinion is that this tragedy coloured the remaining twenty-five years of Quiller Couch's life, and as a result, *Nicky-Nan: Reservist* is seen generally as a 'spirited book', presenting the war effort in a much more kindly light than he was able to muster after his son's death.

Nicky-Nan: Reservist, however, demands a critical re-assessment. Foremost, it is a dialogic novel where competing ideologies are expressed—regarding the war and Cornwall's response to it. The novel is densely written, and in the text, Standard English and Cornu-English dialogue compete for recognition through Quiller Couch's intimate picture of the coastal town of Polpier (obviously based on his family's home village of Polperro). The town is suffering from 'war fever' and in the titular character Nicky-Nan (Nicholas Nanjivell), we discover a man who suffers from 'epitheliomia of the leg',[87] rendering him unable to join up properly, and so he becomes a reservist. This difficulty presents Quiller Couch the facility to then present debate though Nicky Nan, as an individual who 'acts' as a reservist but who has doubts about the conflict. The novel might also be read in the light of James' recent findings on pre-war imperialist English propaganda working on the Cornish,[88] for it is certainly a novel, where seemingly Cornish readerships expect certain behaviours to be encoded and installed into the characters. Through the narrative, these behaviours (such as the use of allotments for the war effort, the building of a military camp and naval test firing) are considered and worked through. The reader is left to watch the 'drama' of the debate unfold before them.

Nicky Nan itself is an interesting name, since it is based on the traditional Cornish festival of 'Nicky Nan Night', an event recorded by Quiller Couch's father, Thomas Quiller Couch in 1855.[89] The festival (traditionally held on the Monday before Lent—and sometimes termed 'Peasen Monday' or 'Hall Monday') licensed the youths of villages to play practical jokes on their neighbours and to indulge in minor acts of vandalism. The night also involved knocking on doors and running away from them before people inside could see who the tricksters were. In some parts of Cornwall, the night was labelled 'Roguery night' presumably because that night led to roguish and boisterous behaviour. In this sense, Quiller Couch's title for the novel is apt, for the central character, is indeed, something of a rogue and out-of-step with the general feeling about the emergent war. We may go further and argue that Nicky Nan indulges in minor 'disagreements' over war policy and activities in the town of Polpier—thus putting him at often anarchic odds with the rest of the community. He works in contrast to much other Anglo-Cornish literature as both an 'insider' and 'outsider' figure.

Many of the debates in the novel regard the effect of the war on the fishery, which was central to the village's economy and sense of being. Nan is a naval reservist, though a somewhat reluctant warrior, who is more at home fishing off the south coast of Cornwall. However, the novel begins with an intersection of this small community with the wider European conflict:

> When news of the War first came to Polpier, Nicholas Nanjivell (commonly known as Nicky-Nan) paid small attention to it, being preoccupied with his own affairs. Indeed, for some days the children knew more about it than he, being tragically concerned in it—poor mites!—though they took it gaily enough. For Polpier lives by the fishery, and of the fishermen a large number— some scores—had passed through the Navy and now belonged to the Reserve. The good fellows had the haziest notion of what newspapers meant by the Balance of Power in Europe, not perhaps could any one of them have explained why, when Austria declared war on Servia [Serbia], Germany should be taking a hand. But they had learnt enough on the lower deck to forebode that, when Germany took a hand, the British navy would soon be clearing for action.[90]

In this small introductory section of the novel there is much of the ideology of the text to be discussed. Initially, Quiller Couch portrays the peripheral status of Cornwall, yet as we read on, it soon becomes clear that the whole of the European continent will be embroiled in the war, and to this extent, peripherality is no excuse. We also learn of the 'age old' and routine connection between the British Navy and the Cornish (embodied perhaps in the proximity of Polpier to the Royal Naval Dockyard at Plymouth), and that in Cornish villages such as Polpier, other men were passing through its ranks in just the same way. 'Some scores' suggests that the numbers joining were not insignificant.

Noticeably, however, there is a class aspect to all of this: Quiller Couch only details those individuals on the lower decks. It seems the Cornish are not presented as officers—a point which links back to the dominance of Cornu-English dialect in the writing. It also perhaps worth reiterating that news of the War really only comes to the village via one medium: that being the newspaper. In such ways, one might argue that Quiller Couch captures the isolation and innocence of this constructed Cornish world. At the same time, because the novel is written retrospectively (with the benefit of the hindsight already achieved by 1915) there are momentary flashes of future warnings, and indeed how the established Methodist-Christian order will be up-ended. In this sequence some recruits are getting ready to sign up:

> The whole town had assembled by this time, a group about each hero. It was a scene that those who witnessed it remembered through many trying days to

come. They knew not at all why their country should be at war. Over the harbour lay the usual Sabbath calm: high on the edge of the uplands stood the outposts of the corn, yellowing to harvest: over all the assured God of their fathers reigned in the August heaven. Not a soul present had harboured one malevolent thought against a single German. Yet the thing had happened: and here, punctually summoned, the men were climbing on board the brakes, laughing, rallying their friends left behind—all going to slay the Germans.[91]

Purposefully Quiller Couch uses the medievalism of the verb 'slay' to reinforce how the enemy will be dealt with, It ironically indicates the use of old-fashioned weapons, such as swords, when, in fact, the war emerging was highly mechanised. Much of the early debate amongst the villagers of the novel is contestation over whether Nicky Nan is faking his injury or 'shamming' (shirking); though it does remain unclear how his leg came to be in the condition. An anonymous and concerned 'Well-wisher' writes to him asking why 'you are not taking your place along with the other men that went off to fight for their country'.[92] A letter arrives from a Registrar in Troy (Quiller Couch's on-going literary imagination of Fowey[93]) to enquire why he shows this 'non-compliance'. Once this matter is settled, the novel then turns to consider the effects of the war effort on the community. A cynic is found in the Cornu-English voice of Benny Rowett who recognises the cost of the effort as well as its effect on maritime (and therefore economic) life:

> "Boo-oom!" echoed Un' Benny Rowett on the Quay, mocking the noise of the cannonade. "War—bloody war, my hearties! There goes a hundred pound of o' taxpayers' money; an' there go all our pilchards for this season, the most promisin' in my recollection."[94]

The novel culminates in more men going off to war, which Nicky-Nan remains cynical about. The dialogic within the text may be too simple for some, but probably Quiller Couch believed in putting before the public the debate and how it affected the working-classes of a Cornish town: the very people the recruitment drivers needed to convince. He does, however, show much more subtlety and awareness than some, by, for example, reinforcing the naval link. It would have been interesting to see how Quiller Couch might have dealt with those Cornishmen who did sign up and marched off to war; particularly because, as a writer, he was particularly aware of class, identity and linguistic issues, which might have formed the subject matter of any novel or short story of his, set during conflict. With *Nicky Nan; Reservist*, he goes some way in beginning this, but perhaps, like Joseph Hocking, Quiller Couch himself had become too much a part of the English establishment. Although partially a text of resistance to the war, in other ways, it is ideologically compliant; complicit with imperial England.

Some years after the novel was first published, in a preface to the 1929 edition, Quiller Couch seemed to undergo the same doubts as Hocking did about the place and purpose of the war. Whilst Nan's cynicism is gently mocked in the novel of 1915, here we see a more recalcitrant and world-weary Quiller Couch; perhaps not only affected by the death of this son, but also by the overwhelming sense of grief that the Great War had given to Cornwall, and to the whole of Western Europe. He seems apologetic for the text:

> My first and last object in adding a preface (or a post-script) to this story, published in 1915, is to ask the reader to make such allowance as he can by setting the clock of his mind back to that dark time. It was written in the intervals of recruiting for a battalion of infantry, and it reflects the anger I must have shared with many at the cruel obstacles to persuasion put in our way by unthinking, and worse than unthinking, people.[95]

Quiller Couch goes on to suggest that he was too critical of the Cornish, and perhaps too, the reservists. However, he still concludes that 'our youngsters had been taught by Church and Chapel that war was anti-Christian', comparing recruitment in Cornwall to that found in English universities where 'boys trained to an ideal of service [and] the difficulty was to deal with the rush of volunteers'.[96] Both points are critical in showing the different responses of both working and middle classes, as well as the difference in attitude in Cornwall and England.

GOING AGAINST THE GRAIN? ROBERT WALLING AND *AN HOULSEDHAS*

Perhaps one of the strangest literary texts to emerge during the First World War is a small set of magazines, written, hand-coloured and produced by the journalist Robert Walling (1895-1976). Only three issues of the magazine *An Houlsedhas [The West]* survive,[97] and in Cornish literary criticism,[98] it has not been much celebrated or discussed. Of late however, Walling's vision for the magazine has been praised,[99] the more so for the fact that it was conceived and written whilst he was recovering from a wound sustained on the Western Front. It is true that Walling was not the conventional Cornish revivalist of this period.[100] Walling and his magazine have not been much studied during the twentieth century—or even discussed in a Cornish Language context—but thanks to the recent biographical efforts of Ann Trevenen Jenkin and Stephen Gadd, we now know more about Walling and his achievements.[101]

He was born in Plymouth, was educated there, and became a reporter on the *Western Daily Mercury*. He did, however, have an interest in the Cornish language, and following study of Henry Jenner's *Handbook of the Cornish Language* (1904),[102] as well as his own research, Walling began to learn and write in the language. Whilst studying in this way, Walling originally became a member of the territorial force of the Royal Garrison Artillery, gaining a commission as Second Lieutenant in April 1913. When war broke out in 1914, his journalistic career was interrupted. He was mobilised on 4 August. In 1916, he was made a Captain, and when wounded and in hospital recovering, began the process of writing the magazines. His intention seems to have been to show what could be done with the language, but also to celebrate past literature too. Had the magazine extended its run to further issues, it would have made a very substantial contribution to the revival of the language. As it stands, we have a tantalising picture of what might have been.

During the conflict Walling was injured once more at the battle of Passchendaele and in 1918 was invalided out of service. He went on to become a highly respected journalist and editor, and in 1934 was made a Bard of the Cornish Gorsedd at a ceremony at Padderbury Top, Menheniot, near Liskeard, where he took the bardic name of *Scryfer an Mor* [Writer of the Sea]. It was obvious that the embryonic Gorsedd knew enough of his achievements in the language to award him with a bardship, but in the correspondences and papers of many of the core revivalists, he is curiously not much mentioned.

In 2016 Gadd prepared a set of very useful translations of Walling's text, and in the volume in which these occur, the reader is given facsimile reproductions of the original text, so that he or she can observe the style and format of the original.[103] Walling's imagining of Cornish drew on a 'classical' Breton style and font,[104] which does provide some difficulties in clarity for the contemporary reader. Clearly however, this was purposeful, since he fully knew the connection between the two languages.[105] Had Cornish a similar model, he may well have chosen this, but even at this early point in the Revival, Walling was seemingly aware of the debate over orthographies within the language.

It seems that the long time spent in hospital afforded Walling the time to work on the magazine. It is not known if further copies of each magazine were made, or whether these are the only 'drafted' survivals. To this reader, and the editors of the recent edition of his work, it would seem that the latter is more likely. To the casual observer, the magazines may initially look slight. The first edition is around twenty-two pages long, the second edition the same length and the third edition shorter at just four pages. The cover of each edition marked the date and carried a hand-drawn coloured sketch of a Cornish landscape; the first seemingly featuring an estuary with a setting sun; the second cliffs and a seascape, again with a setting sun, and Celtic knotwork, whilst the final edition carries an image of a tor, again set within Celtic knotwork. Walling's name—as editor—appears on each of them.

The texts have an interesting history. On visiting Walling in 1976, Cornish-language poet Tim Saunders (b.1952) was given the three surviving copies because Walling felt Saunders would be interested in them.[106] Saunders found the copies fascinating and after reading them, handed them to the Institute of Cornish Studies for preservation. However, the Institute of Cornish Studies had no serviceable library and so they entered the private collection of Professor Charles Thomas (1928-2016) at his library at Lambessow in Truro. Although out of the public domain, their placing in Thomas' personal collection helped to preserve them. This would account for the critical silence upon them.

For the most part, the magazine is dominated by insertions of 'classic' Cornish texts, especially from the 'Late Renaissance' period. However, in the third volume of *An Houlsedhas* Walling does something quite remarkable; he transgresses the dominant pattern. In contrast to the Arthurian and somewhat lamenting literature offered by other early revivalists, Walling offers a focused and taut description of a British tank. Time has meant that the power and innovation of Walling's work here are perhaps more highly valued than ever, since we have a Cornish-language writer completing a literary construction of the war—using modern and technological vocabulary. When one scans the literature generated by other early writers of the revival, rarely do they focus the language on such a contemporary topic.[107] Walling's innovation is therefore absolute. He goes against the grain. Accompanied in the original magazine by a sketch of such a tank (generally known as the Mark 1), in the first part of his description, Walling highlights their dreadful power:

> An 'tank', neb yw mar gerys da kales, yw jynn a vresel ankoth. Pan an Almanyon y'n gwelas an kynsa gweyth yth ens i muskok omstummys hag ownekhes. I re wrussa krysi ev dhe vos mil euthyk nowydh! Ha nyns eus marth dhymm, rag an 'tank' yw, pur wir, pyth wolok ahas hag ownek. Hemma vo orth omladh an 'Somme' mis Gortheren, 1916. Lemmyn, yth yw an 'tankow' aswonys avel arv vreselek pur elwes, ha yth ens i an enthyk-tra besydhys yn Frynk hag yn Flanders.

> [The 'tank', which is so famously invulnerable, is a peculiar war machine. When the Germans saw it for the first time, they were crazed, turning back terrified. They had believed it to be an awful new animal! And that is not a surprise for me, for the tank is indeed a thing of dreadful and frightening appearance. This was the one that was fighting at the 'Somme' in July 1916. Now, 'tanks' are now recognised as much called upon weapons of war, and they were the vulgar things baptised in Frame and in Flanders.][108]

This is a very different use of Cornish than the route most Revivalist writing was going down, which, in effect, was a recapitulation of the Celto-Catholic construct of 'past' Cornwall. Instead, Walling was describing the engineering needed to make the tank operate. In some senses, this work may be seen as a fusion of Cornish language with the technological innovation associated with Cornwall in the industrial revolution (in effect, Joseph Hocking's 'Celtic fire' and 'imaginative race'):

An 'tankow' yw formys a dhur yn liw trog. A vertu usi an 'trackow', avel kadonyw disdiwedhysek: war an re ma, an 'tank' a wra gwaya kepar hag eneval kammfurvek! An 'trackow' yw oberys, dre ger, gans an jynnow-trosek gallose, an re yw gerrys yn an korf. An tothderdegys gans an jynnow may yw ogasti deg mildir yn unn eur war fordh ha namme peswar po pymp mildir yn unn eur dres ves.

[Tanks are made of steel in broken colour. Its advantage is its 'tracks' like never-ending chains: upon these things the tank moves like some malformed animal. The 'tracks' are driven through a gear, by the noisy powerful engines, the ones that are mounted within the body. The engines have a speed of nearly ten miles in an hour on a road, and nearly four or five miles in an hour through a field.][109]

To look at this more critically, perhaps one might argue that in fact Walling did engage with aspects of classic Celticity—particularly in terms of the font chosen and his selection of Celtic knotwork. However, in terms of content, such work may be seen as a radical movement forward for Cornish—especially in terms of how the language later developed, in magazines such as *Eythen* and *An Gannas*,[110] not to mention the various internet sites and discussion forums which have allowed Cornish to become a contemporary European language. In the final part of his description, Walling takes time to examine the weaponry used and how it could defeat German defences:

A vertu, ynwedh, yw dew dron, aval trogow: yma myns kanonyow byghan a denn skav, neb a denn krogan a hwegh penns. Hemm yw an 'tank gour' yn tinnik. An 'tank kansgour' a's teves kanonyow 'Vickers' yn le an 6-penns. Yma kanonyow 'Lewis' dhe oll an 'tankow' a-rag hag a-dhelergh.
An tankow a yll plattya gwiver Almaynek yn heudhek.

[To its advantage, also, are two protuberances [sponsons], like trunks: there are a number of small cannons that fire quickly – that first a shell of six pounds. This is only the 'man tank'. The 'hundred man tank' has 'Vickers' cannons instead of the 6-pounder. There are 'Lewis' cannons on all of the 'tanks', front and rear.
The 'tanks' are able to flatten the German wire with ease.][111]

Again, in this it is interesting to see the war described from a genuinely Cornish linguistic point of view. Such work also pulls into question, the reality of the wider 'British' collective in the war, since it shows that the imagined or constructed Britain was actually made up of component parts, of which the Cornish were a significant group. Perhaps sadly, it seems Walling did not write much more material in Cornish, though he seems to have kept an interest in the revival well into the 1970s. *An Houlsedhas* therefore remains a curious but engaging example of how the language may have taken a different turn during this phase. Had more material been shaped along these lines, then maybe the language would be seen as less elitist and idealised, and in fact, show the reality of modern warfare and human wastage. Again, within its pages we see a combination of romance of the Celtic past and the Celtic 'West' but strikingly, also too, the reality of the situation on the Western Front.

DULCE ET DECORUM EST PRO PATRIA MORI: POETIC IMAGININGS OF THE GREAT WAR

As noted earlier, poetic imaginings of the First World War are somewhat scant when compared to the apparent wider picture in Britain. When considering the poets of the Cornish Revival, it is Walling that we first turn to. Alongside copies of *An Houlsedhas*, in 1976 Walling also presented Saunders with a single, unpublished poem in manuscript form, which was titled *War Lerch an Bresel [After the War]*.[112] The exact textual history of this piece is difficult to discover, though presumably given Walling's interest in the conflict and his contribution to the development of *An Houlsedhas*, it is presumably the end of the Great War that is being marked. Like most of the early poetry of the Revival, the poem's rhyme scheme is relatively simple, and the poem decidedly short, but we know that this is the way in which 'recovering' literatures often work.[113] In essence, such pieces are experimental 'work-outs' with the language—to see what can be accomplished:

> Gwel yu'n broniou heb huelbren
> Gwel yu'n awel heb an gwez,
> Gwel es clowans cledh po'n omladh
> Yu coseleth en an lez .
> Gwrenz an costennow a tweder
> A'ueh da gregi war an gwâl,
> Bednes gortos cledh an wain,
> Tawas a dhur rudh ha dâl

> [Better are the hills without the beacon,
> better is the wind without the cry,

   better than hearing sword or fighting
is quietness in the court.
Let the thick shields
be hung above on the wall,
let the sword remain in the sheath,
let its red and blind steel remain silent.][114]

Here, Walling's poem almost has a commanding, quasi-religious tone (probably much influenced by his knowledge of Breton literature and culture), where the poet is watching over the unnerving quiet of the deserted battlefield. It certainly captures the wastefulness of the conflict; something that we know Walling observed first hand. However, the imagery of the poem is medieval, even heroic, with the notions of 'Celtic' warriors of old, laying down their swords (connecting back to Quiller Couch's construct of 'slaying'). Thus, there is within the lament, a romanticized tone which connects such work to the implicit 'Medievalism' of the Revival. Perhaps compared to the realism contained in *An Houlsedhas* about the mechanistics of the conflict, here Walling resorts to Revivalist type. Nonetheless, the poem still has an inherent power with the romantic metaphors standing for the huge casualties suffered.

Given the romantic metaphor of 'knights' serving for 'greater good', it is curious that within Anglo-Cornish and Cornish literature, there is not more heroic Arthurian-influenced literature from this time. One might have expected that poets and perhaps playwrights might well have drawn upon the ethos of King Arthur facing off a new evil in the form of Germany and her allies. With a run of literature emerging in the late nineteenth century and a further flourish in the 1920s and 1930s (specifically because of Revivalist and tourist interests at Tintagel[115]), it feels like the period from 1910 to 1920 (the decade in which the Great War is located), as Hale, Kent and Saunders have shown, very little Arthurian-influenced literature emerges.[116] This position is a curious one, since history has demonstrated that when conflict emerges, often countries draw upon culturally heroic figures.[117] Therefore, for those involved in the conflict from Cornwall, it is somewhat odd that the Arthurian matter is not more extensively drawn upon for inspiration.

In particular, this is at odds with some of the key findings of James' research who argues that before the conflict, British society was preparing the youth of the constituent parts of the country to be ready for war.[118] This, she argues, was instilled via books depicting heroic characters (such as King Arthur and Robin Hood), through the scouting and volunteer movements and via a general call to do one's duty. James thus concludes that these imperial materials were not only put in place by the establishment because it knew war was coming, but also because such 'invention' would allow for the call to arms from the constituent groups—who would by then have been manipulated enough to enlist as an 'English' response. That the project seems to have discontinued within the war perhaps again shows the futility of the conflict and maybe even that the Cornish response was actually to 'savour' their returning King Arthur. It may also be that Arthur was finding his purpose in new ways—as an ideological figure within the Cornu-Celtic Revival.

Just as the Cornish (particularly in the china-clay mining region of mid-Cornwall) initially saw the conflict as an 'English war' their divided sense of loyalty (reinforced by centuries of English imperialism)—on the one hand Cornish; on the other English[119]—writers in opening decades of the twentieth century had to cope with these paradoxes of identity.[120] History and identity were not top of the list of priorities for most working-class people in Cornwall, and at this stage, only a few seemingly 'fringe' and frankly 'odd' middle-class Revivalists and antiquarians had the audacity to put Cornish identity on an equal footing to English identity (and to other Celtic peoples). We know that most Cornish who emigrated in the late nineteenth and early twentieth centuries were generally also regarded as being English.[121] It is therefore not surprising to find in Anglo-Cornish poetry a similar sense of divided loyalty. If we do follow James' position, then this kind of response might be seen as a similar strand of successful imperial manipulation.

The major Anglo-Cornish poet James Dryden Hosken (1861-1953) is representative of this 'confusion' and collision of identities at this point. Born in Helston, Hosken rose to fame in the tail-end of the nineteenth century; his poetic dramas informed by Greek Tragedy and by dramatic and celebrated English literary figures such as Christopher Marlow. As the Celtic Revival emerged in Cornwall though, Hosken saw the potential and wrote a number of poems inspired by places and by legends and myths. The result of this was that eventually he was to be made a bard at the first Cornish Gorsedd at Boscawen Ûn stone circle in 1928.[122] During the war however, he seems to have had divided loyalties for his poetic work then embraced a wider England fighting against a foe. It is perhaps hard for modern observers (especially those of Cornish-nationalist persuasion) to see the place of this kind of writing, but once we go beyond the issues of identity, we begin to see Hosken writing verse of an inspirational and buoyant nature when it came to the question of patriotism. A particular problematical poem in regard to this issue is 'To the Spirit of England'—collected in an anthology in 1928 (matching the year of his bardship)—but probably written during or, in the immediate decade after the Great War:

Arise, my country, as of old you rose

69

When in titanic might Napoleon flew
His banners, and in stern defence drew
His conquering sword against you—other foes
Now threaten you, and from a man's hand grows
A mighty cloud: but you can proudly view
A thousand years of battle where they sue
For peace and mercy who provoke your blows.
 Even as Rome stood when Hannibal drew near
 Or when the savage Gaul fell back in awe
Before her silent senators in state;
So stand my country guiltless of a fear,
Sure of your own great heart and of that law
Marked out for you, but by no human fate.[123]

Perhaps the unpalatable nature of the poem for modern observers—not only because of its inherent Anglicization but also its blind patriotism—makes it one of the most difficult texts for us to examine. The only way we are able to deal with it is to think of the contribution that Cornwall is making to this wider effort. This is fine to an extent, but Hosken perhaps was a writer (like Hocking) not prepared enough for the casualty rate that followed. Some readers will also, no doubt, note his approach to the 'savage Gaul' and see the similarities between how Celtic culture and Gaulish culture were viewed by the Romans. Earlier union against Napoleon is also referred to here, and we recognise that the poem is embedded with contradictions and confusion. At the same time, its message was perhaps needed to encourage or to reflect upon the war effort. Readers may be dissuaded to read more of Hosken by this poem, but a scan through his other writings show his commitment to Cornish culture, and poetic celebration of it. This poem, however, stands as symbolic of the wider confusion over identity that, if we are honest, still persists in some Cornish people's minds.[124]

A poet from later in the twentieth century who composed lines reflecting upon the First World War was Jack G. Jolly (1920-2003). Jolly was born in Stithians and brought up in Lanner. He joined the Devon and Cornwall Light Infantry during the Second World War, serving in India. Poetry remained something he wrote throughout his life, whilst working away, and on returning to Cornwall in 1960, he completed a considerable amount of work which was assembled into an anthology in 2010. His poem *Melopomene's Men* is his tribute to the poets who wrote about the conflict. Melopomene (most often spelt Melpomene) was the Greek Muse of Tragedy; thus, Jolly was inciting a classically-inspired figure into the concept behind his poem. The piece has a ballad-like simplicity with the third, fourth and fifth lines of each stanza being repeated throughout, giving the whole a rhythmic, almost marching quality. Jolly knew men who had served during the First World War and thus his conversations with them, what he knew about the conflict, and his own experiences of serving overseas make up the poem's content. Here are both the first and final stanzas of the poem:

Melopomene
Had a battalion rare
The sweetest songs they sang
Were bitter-sweet

Over there, over there.

The singers gone
To deaths beyond compare
The sweetest songs they sang
Were bitter-sweet

Over there, over there.[125]

Compared to Hosken, Jolly is not a well-known poet within Anglo-Cornish writing but his instincts in writing about the Great War as a tragedy seems symbolically apt. Indeed, the Cornish poetic position is much like that seen elsewhere; that here was a tragedy of unfathomable proportions, which should never be seen again: the misplaced idea that his was 'the war to end all wars'—seen through at times, a more Cornish lens. As Philip Payton demonstrates elsewhere in this volume, poets such as R. J. Noall also dallied with constructions of the war in verse, as in 'Sweet Rosa Trethowan of Fair Constantine'. Although sentimental, and as Payton notes, 'not great literature', such verse showed the effect of the War in the popular imagination of the Cornish.

HAIL AGAIN OUR NATIVE SHORE: STORIED SONG AND FOLKLORE

Often in Cornwall, literature and song collide and fuse; one only has to look at Robert Stephen Hawker's *Trelawny: The Song of the Western Men*, or the anonymous Cornish-language text *Strawberry Leaves [Delkiow Sevi]*.[126] Actually, *Trelawny* was often sung by regiments within the Duke of Cornwall's Light Infantry on both the training grounds and in battle. One of the other songs that was popular during the First World War was 'The Old "One and All"', which, according to Dunstan, during the conflict, became the 'Old Cornwall Regimental March'.[127] This would have been performed and sung at the barracks in Bodmin, but also where the Cornwall Light Infantry fought between 1914 and 1918.[128] The song, however, had earlier roots. It was composed by Lieutenant–Colonel Willyams for the

Royal Cornwall Rangers Militia in 1811, who volunteered to serve in Ireland. At this point in time, George III made the militia a Light Infantry Regiment and the song seemed to represent this transition and acknowledgement of their military prowess. Dunstan comments less upon the lyrical foundation of the song. It would appear though that some of the words he recorded in 1932 were derived from its earlier usage, as noted in the final verse:

> But when the din of war is o'er
> Our services required no more
> We'll hail again our native shore,
> With "One and All",
> And then the Cornish Volunteer
> Shall meet kind welcome, and hearty cheer;
> Plenty of beef and good, strong beer:
> Drink "One and All."
> Then let the bells of Bodmin ring
> The Cornish-Irish lads shall sing
> Drink to their sweethearts and their King
> Drink "One and All"![129]

Although the above song has its roots in older Cornish culture, the events of the First World War ensured that it was used in a new way, and in effect, reinvented for the soldiers serving in the present. Similar adaptations were made to the ritualised theatre of the Obby Oss festival held in Padstow on 1 May to mark the return of summer. The origins of much of the ceremony are lost in time, and are speculated upon by a number of observers.[130] The origin of the "Blue Ribbon Oss" is much more readily associated with the ending of the First World War. In the late nineteenth century the "Blue Oss" was supported by members of the town's Temperance Movement. This was because they wanted to discourage the consumption of alcohol on May Day, which was associated with the activities of the "Old" or "Red Oss". However, after the First World War, the importance of Temperance as a social force faded and the newer oss become known as the "Peace Oss", to mark the ending of the conflict. It is widely known that each oss has a 'stable' (in the case of the "Old Oss", this is the Golden Lion Inn and the "Blue Ribbon or Peace Oss", the Institute, from which they emerge at the start of May Day's proceedings and retire at the end. Usually, in the late afternoon, the osses meet at the maypole and dance together.

According to Rawe, the new Peace Oss was constructed in 1919 by young men who had returned from service.[131] It was slightly larger than the Old Oss, and during its time has raised thousands of pounds for charity. The Peace Oss also visited the Royal Albert Hall in 1927 in a display of

Cornish culture. It would seem that at present the two osses sing similar versions of the songs associated with the festival; a situation which perhaps contradicts their different origins.

LITERARY LIVES IN KERNOW: THE GREAT WAR'S INFLUENCE ON LITERARY AUTOBIOGRAPHY

The origins of other writers connected to the First World War are perhaps documented more readily. Cultural-Materialist criticism is contentious when it comes to traditional biographical criticism (and, needless to say, an approach based on autobiographical writing) because of the former's political commitment and because it puts emphasis on textual analysis and context, not just the life of the writer.[132] However limiting 'archetypal' biographical criticism and literary autobiography are—particularly in terms of its 'liberal humanist' approach to literature and to the specific links between an author's life and his or her texts—it is still acknowledged in some quarters (and by myself) that it is an appropriate method of enquiry.[133]

As the reader will note, one has to be very careful assigning particular moments in an author's life to how his or her literature develops—simply because the latter may not, in fact, be related to the former. This is why Cultural Materialism usually resists such a methodology. In a chapter devoted to how Cornish and Anglo-Cornish literature has responded to the First World War we should, however, perhaps acknowledge its influence on the lives, and therefore according to biographical criticism, the writings of that particular poet, novelist or dramatist. It should be acknowledged that sometimes autobiographical writing can be read with an eye on context and historical moment of production, so in our survey, there may well be opportunity and justification for appropriate scrutiny of them.

A major figure in twentieth-century Anglo-Cornish literature was the poet and novelist Jack Clemo.[134] Clemo, who died in 1994, was born in 1916 in the middle of the First World War. He was therefore a writer born too young to write directly about the experiences of the war. However, in his biographical writings there are several mentions of the conflict; in particular related to his father Reginald (Reggie) Clemo. As demonstrated in Thompson's recent biography, Clemo was highly critical of his father, both in terms of his move to America for 'materialist' reasons and because he indulged in the use of prostitutes there.[135] Clemo's eventual belief, of course, was that the 'Devil had rendered him unfit for marriage', but that he would fight against this and eventually realise his own 'mystical-erotic' quest with Ruth Peaty.[136] The key point is that much of Clemo's literary output was supposedly stimulated by his reaction to his father's behaviour—causing Clemo to develop hereditary syphilis (eventually leading to blindness and deafness)—and because of his father's untimely death.

Reggie Clemo had, in fact, returned to Britain to work, and in late 1916 he was called up to train at the Plymouth base HMS Vivid II. By 30 October 1917, he was serving aboard the destroyer HMS Tornado shovelling coal into its engines.[137] On escort in the North Sea, the ship was torpedoed on 22 December and sank on the 23. Working in the engine rooms, Reggie would not have had a hope of surviving. According to Clemo, a telegram arrived to inform the family of his death on Christmas Day. The loss of his father, and then his later learning of how his sexual life had influenced Clemo's own health might be read as crucial in terms of the writer's formative years. In his autobiography, *Confession of a Rebel* (1949) Clemo was to reflect on the influence of this moment:

> When the first shock and prostration had passed, my mother groped her way back to the security of what she had left, the source of strength and guidance that had never failed in the old home. While many women of her generation yielded their senses to the usage of disillusion and revolt, she turned aside—as I was to turn aside from my generation in the nineteen-thirties—to discover in a full surrender to Christ what His purpose might be, and to shrink from no sacrifice in co-operating with that purpose.[138]

Clemo seems to advance his own view here that his 'rebellion' (as well as his mother's) was different to the rest of the generation left after the First World War and that the 'disillusion and revolt' (perhaps in terms of losing faith and embracing secularisation) would not be his mother's, nor Clemo's way of proceeding.[139] This view (which is further explained in his biography) set the agenda for Clemo's writing over the next fifty years. Of course, had Reggie lived, there would have been the inevitable confrontation over his behaviour and actions (these crucially remained unresolved for Clemo), but his death in the war also influenced the young Clemo's mentality: his approach to life, death and faith, as witnessed in both his fiction and poetry.[140] The 'rebellion'—made much of in his biography—may be seen as a counter-reaction to the way in which most of society dealt with the tragedy of the First World War. Whilst the war took people towards constructs of Modernism and Secularization, Clemo's reaction was to retreat, firstly into Calvinism and Spiritualism, and later, into Catholicism.[141] In this sense, Clemo is a profoundly 'un-modern' poet and the First World has been a central part of shaping him.

A further observation may be made here with regard to Clemo's earliest literary output. These were his dialect tales published locally in the *Cornish Guardian* newspaper. In their provincial subject matter and Cornu-English, there are perhaps elements of them which represent Cornwall in the post-war period.[142] The texts often rely on the collision of modernism with the way things have been done in the past. Their sense of 'making do' and having to get on with things despite events and lack of hope, perhaps draw on an underlying strand in the post-war period.

The Anglo-Cornish poet, short story writer and historian, A. L Rowse, was born in 1903, and so at the start of the First World War, he was eleven years old. Rowse, as Ollard, and Payton detail, was born at Tregonissey, near St Austell. He was the son of Richard Rowse, a china clay worker, and Annie (née Vanson). Despite his parents being poor and semi-illiterate, he won a place at St Austell Grammar. Rowse was studious and hardworking, and in 1921 won a scholarship to Christ Church, Oxford. He was encouraged to pursue an academic career by his fellow Cornish writer, Arthur Quiller Couch, who became aware of his abilities. The paths that Rowse and Clemo took were very different: the former moved into academia, while the latter was 'stuck' in working-class surrounds. The two writers also differed in their responses to the First World War. Whilst Clemo was too young to remember its impact (beyond his father's death), Rowse was more aware of activity and its reportage. His personal knowledge of it, as well as later learning of its consequences and significance in 'British history' no doubt contributed to the formation of Rowse as a historian. It appears, however, to have had less direct effect on him as a poet.

As his biographers note, one of Rowse's lifelong themes in his academic books and articles was his condemnation of the National Government's policy of appeasement in the 1930s and the economic and political consequences for Great Britain of fighting a second war with Germany.[143] Rowse's views on this were, of course, shaped by his knowledge of the First World War. Within the context of his historical writings it is also worth bearing in mind, that in texts such as *Tudor Cornwall* and *The Expansion of Elizabethan England*, Rowse can now be seen as a pioneer of the new British historiography (and by connection, the 'new Cornish historiography') that recognizes the cultural differences of the constituent parts of the British Isles.[144] This view is now impacting on how historians see the response of the constituent parts to the First World War. His responses to the conflict are first recorded in one of Rowse's most famous works, *A Cornish Childhood*—originally published in 1942. In his description of village life, Rowse writes:

The War—till lately 'the War' still meant in these parts the Great War of 1914 to 1918: evidence perhaps of the slowness of adaptation, tenacity of our minds—the War brought all that life of habit to a sudden full stop, held it suspended, breathless for a full four years in the shadow of its wing, and meanwhile set in motions and tendencies which came to full flood the moment the War was over and swept away the old landmarks in a tide of change. I remember the momentary return to the old ways, for we celebrated the Armistice with a Flora dance through the town. There was something instinctive, pathetic about it, like a gesture remembered from some former existence, which had not meaning anymore.[145]

Although a relatively short sequence at the beginning of the autobiography, there is much we learn about both Rowse's and Cornwall's response to the war. Rowse is well known for his somewhat 'love-hate' relationship with the territory, and there is something of that here. He seems concerned about the 'motions and tendencies' which have been ushered in by the conflict, but also recognizes the impossibility of halting this change. Modernity and Modernism appear to clash with an older agrarian, perhaps even more 'Celtic' way of doing things. Rowse names the dance a Flora Dance.[146] In all likelihood, this would perhaps have been a similar style of Cornish processional dance, which is, of course, at odds with the brutality and catastrophe of the conflict itself.

Throughout his life, Rowse is often aware of his 'Celticity' colliding and jarring against wider English culture,[147] but at the same time, he is sometimes celebratory of the imperial ideal, and dismissive of the narrow-minded views of the Cornish. This is what Payton terms his 'paradoxical Patriotism', but in all likelihood, his hatred of provincialism was also related to his homosexuality. At Oxford, this was more acceptable, whilst in Methodist Cornwall during this time it was not.[148] The fact that Rowse begins the biography with the end of the Great War is also significant. It suggests that his growth toward adulthood will be related to the responses to the conflict and its aftermath. The chapter then laments the old ways that he mentions, as Rowse recounts activities in the ritual year, in farming and in mining. However, this reflection is punctuated by images of those lost or who have served during the war. The writing is even more personal at this point, because these are young men that he knew:

But where are the voices of those young men who sang? Some of them extinguished for ever in the Great War, at the bottom of the North Sea, in France, in Flanders, in Palestine, for those Cornish lads were in all those theatres of the War. Some of them who died were at school with me: I recognized their names on a tablet outside the little chapel at Bethel the other day when walking that way.[149]

Here, of course, Rowse realises the global impact of the Cornish within the First World War and understands their place within the conflict. He is aware of the loss, the sense of wasted lives, and the understanding that those just above him at school were thrown into the war. One of the men at the bottom of the North Sea was Reggie Clemo. The discussion of the tablet re-connects us with the arguments made at the beginning of this article: about the wish for lasting monuments to the fallen. Already here,

Rowse is differentiating the constituent parts of the armed response to
Germany and her allies. Issues related to the war continued to play on
Rowse's mind and his autobiography offers some exact dates, alongside
some very personal experiences of the conflict in his school-books:

> A recruiting march of the D.C. L. I. about district May 8th 1915 is next
> described: might write a local history of the early stages of the War from this
> exercise-book. At Lane End the headmaster joined the officers, some of whom
> made speeches: 'one recruit volunteered, whose name was Mr. Chubb, Poor
> lad, he came back minus a leg from the War. At the end of the day, seventy
> men came forward and offered their services for their King, and were
> accepted'.[150]

Rowse also confesses how patriotic he was at this time and his
schoolbook records some of this energy:

> I was very patriotic. There are 'compositions', i.e. short essays, on St George's
> Day and Empire Day, a letter to British prisoners of war beginning, 'We are all
> sorry to hear that British prisoners are in a state of semi-starvation'. Then
> comes a letter to Count Zeppelin, a very rhetorical work written 'three days
> after the last raid. You think that we English subjects are frightened at such
> atrocities that, through you, have been committed... But beware! I say, there is
> a greater trial and you will suffer. There is still more oracular remonstrance
> addressed to 'His Imperial Majesty, the Emperor of Germany: 'I have
> addressed you by your full coronation title; but you are not worthy of such an
> honour'.[151]

Here, not only does the imperial propaganda placed on the Cornish
seem to have worked (this is from an autobiography very explicitly titled *A
Cornish Childhood*, but once again, we see the early Rowse developing
both in a literary and a political sense. His address to the Emperor of
Germany matches the fictionalisation occurring in the fiction of Joseph
Hocking. Later, when describing his time at Secondary School, Rowse
further reflects on the quietness of the village during the War:

> The impression of a profound peace was added to by the absence of the men
> away on service, the increasing desertedness of town and village of traffic and
> men alike.[152]

What is interesting here is that Rowse notes the progression from 1916
onwards of how many men had enlisted and this result in the shutdown of
activity. It must have been a very haunting process. The second half of the
biography concentrates on Rowse's scholarship, his arrival at Oxford, the
lights of which 'held my eyes ever since'.[153] He did begin with the War in
the autobiography but crosses it as he continues in the account. On the
whole, the First World War sequences are not substantial ones, but this

historical moment continued to influence Rowse in his later work.[154] Rowse was actually quite an extensive war poet himself but his focus as a poet remains solely on the Second World War.[155]

It is perhaps impossible to deal with Clemo and Rowse without dealing with the other major Anglo-Cornish poet of this era: Charles Causley. Causley—born in 1917—wrote only one major autobiographical work; this was *Hands to Dance and Skylark* (1951), which detailed his time during the Navy in the Second World War.[156] As mentioned earlier, his poetic and theatre works make him resoundingly a writer of that later conflict. However, as detailed in Green's bibliography of Causley, his father (Charlie Causley) died in 1924 from long-standing injuries sustained from the First World War.[157] Charlie served in the Royal Army Service Corps. He had held the rank of Driver (equivalent to Private), and, having worked as a gardener and groom, was in charge of horses. He served in the Battle of the Somme in 1916 where he lost a finger. Green speculates that he could have been holding a horse's head when the horse jerked and pulled off a finger, as this was a common injury.[158] At some point, however, Charlie was gassed and later developed pulmonary pneumonia. He was discharged from the army being 'of no further use' but died at No.18 St Stephen's Hill, Launceston, when Charles was seven. His name is recorded on the War Memorial in the town. Largely because of this, Causley had to leave school at fifteen to earn money for the family, working as an office boy during his early years. It was only when he was older that he could train as a teacher. It seems that for the above reasons, in 2017, Green was able to make the following assessment:

> The Great War had an enormous influence on Causley when it came to joining up. His father's experience and staying in Crownhill in Plymouth opposite a barracks turned him against the army and he opted instead for the navy. Causley hated the winter and being cold and wet and so the 'Poor Bloody Infantry' was not for him. He was also very much influenced by the later Great War poets, men such as Ivor Gurney, Isaac Rosenberg, and especially David Jones. There is a David Jones print in Causley's bedroom. These three very influential poets all served in the ranks in the infantry. Causley was very politically aware and could see the Second World War coming. In the late 1930s he read an article about Hitler's concentration camps in the Reader's Digest. Some of W. H. Auden's poems alerted him too.[159]

Therefore, although missing the direct experience of the War himself (he was only three years old when the war finished), Causley did witness his father's decline and death from the War's consequences. Perhaps the biographical critic would make a direct connection here to later works by Causley, such as 'Nursery Rhyme of Innocence and Experience'—which perhaps fuses his experiences of the effects of both wars:

'O where is the sailor
 With bold red hair?
 And what is that volley
 On the bright air?

'O where are the other
 Girls and boys?
 And why have you brought me
 Children's toys?[160]

The poem recalls the experiences of a young boy who grows up while
the sailor is away fighting at war. The sailor does not return but a friend of
his still gives the boy the toys he asked for. Time has passed and the boy,
now grown up, has no need for them, but does now understand the
consequences of war. The poem is one of the finest Anglo-Cornish war
poems ever written. It would thus appear that although Cultural-Materialist
criticism may wish to deny the importance of biographical style criticism,
clearly in these three writers there are core connections between their
family histories and their work. Most interestingly perhaps, in the lives of
Clemo and Causley, we see how the death of their fathers was a key part in
the shaping of them as poets; a drama matched in Rowse by his awareness
of those lost at war directly from the Higher Quarter community around St
Austell.

DRAMATISING THE CORNISH IN THE GREAT WAR

It might be argued that of all the Celtic territories it is Cornwall that has
developed the most profound and interesting drama over the centuries.[161]
Although it may have competition with Ireland in the twentieth century,[162]
threads of dramatic literature were established early on in communities in
Cornwall, and these have continued ever since.[163] Populist, community-
orientated and often located outdoors or in site-specific venues, theatre in
Cornwall stands as one of the territory's most popular and lasting art-
forms. Kershaw, Craig, and Kent have all argued for the way in which
theatre works in Cornwall as a mechanism of cultural intervention and how
it can operate in setting up a space for dialogic work—where competing
identities and ideologies (in essence, those which both Quiller Couch and
Rowse identified) are explored—with the audience left to decide which one
they approve of.[164]

It is therefore perhaps somewhat logical that the Great War would find
its way into theatre and be depicted dramatically. Although it would appear
that few dramas from Cornwall were written in the immediate aftermath of
the war, towards the end of the twentieth century and at the start of the
twenty first, it has been fruitful subject matter for several dramatists and

theatre companies. I write, of course here, as something of a participant observer; an uneasy position for any scholar, but one that is necessary in order to view the full range of work developed.

A significant text from the late twentieth century was *Where Are You Gone, Jimmy Trevenna?* (1996) by Simon Turley.[165] Turley is not Cornish by birth but has an affinity with the territory. He was born in Bristol in 1958, and grew up in Somerset, eventually reading English at the University of Cambridge. In the 1980s, while wishing to find a teaching position in Cornwall, he gained a teaching post at Eggbuckland School in Plymouth, and worked there for some twenty years, before moving to write professionally, and to teach part-time. Liaison with the Barbican Theatre in Plymouth allowed Turley to develop many theatre-in-education projects. *Where Are You Gone, Jimmy Trevenna?* was premiered at Eggbuckland School (in itself interesting, since it is rare for a Cornu-centric text to be performed in Plymouth, especially in a school), and was later revived in 2001 by the Young Company at the Theatre Royal in Plymouth—subsequently also being produced at the 2003 Edinburgh Festival, by the Trevenna Theatre Company, and in 2008, at the Ridgeway School in Plymouth.

Set during the First World War, the play considers the impact of the conflict on a small fishing community in Cornwall called St Nevin. Turley understands well aspects of Cornish difference. In a very telling scene at the beginning of the play, the character David is encountering Kitty Trevenna in the 'horn of strangers'. The debate over identity matches the wider political debate over Cornwall's involvement. On recruitment and enlisting the Cornish were themselves being 'spiky':

Lucy:	They aren't strangers to us.
David:	And, to be sure, I think I never saw a more handsome couple than your brother and that striking girl.
Tim:	Now, now.
Lucy:	Kitty Trevenna.
David:	Trevenna! Even the names here are spiky with poetry.[166]

This is exquisite and adept writing, demonstrating Turley's concern with the insider/outsider theme familiar with much post-war Anglo-Cornish writing, but also a sensitivity and understanding of space and place: somewhat ironic in that the play has never actually been performed in Cornwall itself. Turley is perhaps less comfortable imagining a Cornu-English linguistic world: the characters tend to speak in Standard English. However, issues of identity are at the forefront of the thematic concerns of the play, as seen in this sequence:

| David: | But what an extraordinary thing to say. |

Maria:	What?
David:	He said that he couldn't claim to be Cornish.
Tim:	That's right.
David:	You were born here, weren't you?
Lucy:	And our father was born here too.
David:	What more do they want![167]

The 'they' here is the Cornish, and such a debate over Cornish identity was entering the academy,[168] just as it was being dramatized. As can be seen from these sequences, Turley's style is very fast-paced, and characters rarely give monologues. Inevitably, the opening scenes look at life in the village before the war (exploring the bizarre and comedic sport of 'cow-tipping'), while the later scenes look at events after the conflict has begun. Innocence and experience are thus contrasted.[169] The concept of 'tipping' also facilitates the Cornish characters to use this as a metaphor for getting their own back on imperial oppression: it is the empire writing back at the English. Jimmy's encounter with an angel ordains him as special, and following a kiss from the angel, he is set on his life's course: a tragic trajectory.

Turley integrates moments of Cornish language. Despite it not being historically correct, the teacher Nancy has a dispute over her wish to teach the children Cornish.[170] The cultural-nationalist position is embodied in the character of Albert, who while out fishing with Jimmy swears that he hears 'the ghost of An Gof I warrant... An Gof come agathering us up to go and tip the English...'[171] Such imaginings of Cornwall may well be unrealistic, but this perhaps does not matter: Turley is re-inventing a Cornwall where this position can happen or is at least felt. The transitional device of the village hall dance allows Turley to have a large ensemble on stage, while the conflict ('You know as well as I it *is* an English war'.[172]) is created with tableaux and sound effects.

Ironically, of course, Turley's piece would completely suit the kind of touring theatre which had been established in Cornwall in the post-war period—given this environment of the village hall. Turley's text is, however, ambitious. At its best; for example, at Jimmy's death, when the Angel and Jimmy talk in Cornish and in English (Jimmy: Thought I might get away with Cornish. But you swims like a seal in every language. Angel: *Pengevig osta* [You're a prince], Jimmy Trevenna.[173]) one sees the true possibilities of contemporary theatre about Cornwall. Turley's voice is not well-known but his writing is significant. Certainly, his examination of the First World War is psychologically challenging, offering a vision of ethnic difference in response to the conflict. Like the other plays of the period that were to follow, high tragedy (of the kind identified by the Anglo-Cornish poet Jack G. Jolly) is combined with much comedy.

Of these modern era plays, one that seems to have made considerable impact was my own 2009 work, *Surfing Tommies*.[174] Produced by Bish Bash Bosh Productions and directed by John Hoggarth, the text was toured successfully in Cornwall, and well as completing a Britain-wide tour, proving that explicitly Cornish material could be as successful on stage in non-Cornish locations.[175] The play, in essence, fuses two core aspects of Cornish experience: that of surfing and of serving one's country in wartime. The narrative of the play is conducted through the researches of a modern-day History student (Maisie Pascoe) at the Combined Universities of Cornwall at Tremough, and it explores the lives of three core soldiers of the Duke of Cornwall's Light Infantry. As miners, the soldiers were specifically assigned tunnelling duties, and it is whilst they are in the trenches that they encounter a South African soldier who informs them about surfing.

Once the war is over, the soldiers return home, with the narrative here based on the oral recollections of veteran Perranporth surfer Tom Tremewan's grandfather. Tremewan had explained to me that the first surfers at Perranporth used coffin lids as boards. The irony of this— compounded by the death seen on the Western Front made for an evocative consideration of an 'origin story' for surfing, as well as a unique look at Cornish experience in the war. The play's tragedy is compounded by the shell-shock (now post-traumatic stress disorder) and desertion of its youngest trooper, John Henry Pascoe, who eventually is shot at dawn.[176] One core scene in the play is where John Henry's mother, Rose Pascoe receives the news that her son is dead. She shares this news with John Henry's fiancé:

> An' the pity that do go with ut. People do avoid 'ee, like they'm afraid ov 'ee, when you need they moast. I knaw why. It's cuz they'm scared t'say the wrong thing. So I thanked the man from Telegraphy. "Thank you," I said, and I was down on the beach. There wudn' a soul there, from up Penhale t'Droskyn. An' I knew what I 'ad to do. I 'ad to go up Garnbargus and tell the maid. Close an' sticky that day. I wuz blawed time I   got there. She was out bringin' in the cows fur milking. A lot of flies, I knaw   tha'. An' the cows—all beautiful, dark, loving eyes and slobber, as they comed down off the moor. All fulla' bussy milk fur their calves. She didn' need tellun' neither. Just by me being there— turnin' up out of the blue—she knew. An' 'er face, dear ov 'er. Pain went into ut that day. All she cud do wuz sit down and cry, an' the cows comed down, an' circled us. An' when we sobbed together, we scared them a bit... An' as we held each other, then ut started t'rain... so we'm sat there, holding each other, in the mud.[177]

Hopefully here the Cornu-English language of the monologue expresses a very 'Cornish' sense of loss. Other symbols in the text link to the conflict in the trenches that the Duke of Cornwall's Light infantry were facing: the pun on 'blawed' linking to textual choices elsewhere in the play where individuals were 'blawed up' as well as the ending of the speech linking these two characters to those in the trenches via the imagery of the mud. Interestingly, however, the pathos of this is also combined with much comedy: mainly between Jimmy 'Dunkey'Tamblyn (an awkward, loud and lumpen miner and soldier and his by-the-book 'Cap'n' William Tresawna. When Tamblyn signs up after a recruiting drive from a constructed Joseph Hocking, in order to escape Tresawna at the mine, he is flabbergasted to find that Tresawna will also captain his regiment. In the drama, the two spar, but also end up saving each other.

The work integrated much other First World War culture from Cornwall. One of the lead characters is Robert Walling, the author of *An Houlsedhas*, and he spends much of his time speaking in Cornish. He is changed slightly here and works as a journalist reporting on the front and documenting the experiences of the Cornish 'diggers' as they work in the tunnels. Walling's appearance in the play re-ignited much interest in his writings during the First World War, resulting in the above volume compiling *An Houlsedhas*, which emerged in 2016. Indeed, the final lament of the play in which all of the characters turn to the west [*an Houlsedhas*], to commemorate the war dead, is completed in Cornish—and combined with a poppy wreath mounted on a surfboard, it made for an extremely powerful ending to the play:

Jimmy and William stand next to Robert Walling. The Girl is in front of Robert. All of them face the projection of the ocean, with their backs to the audience.

Robert In memory of all the young men of Cornwall who lost their lives in the Great War. [reads] A Dhew ollgallosek ha tregeredhus, neb a dhisquedhas dhyn dre sacrifis Dha Unvap an hens dhe vudhygolyeth war beghes ha'n bedh, a leun golon y commendyen dhe'th hwith ha'th cur Jy mebyon an blu ma neb a geskerdhas bys y'n houlsedhas yn myttin aga dedhyow. Gront dhedha a'th torn ollgallosek le ha hanow nefra a bes, ha budhygolyeth war vresel kepar del waynsys Jy budhygolyeth war Ankow y honen. A hemma y'th pysyn yn hanow Dha Unvap agan Arluth Yesu Crist. Amen.

All Amen.

Jimmy [as an aside to Robert] Beautiful tha' Mr Walling. Didn' understand a word ov ut – but beautiful all the same.

Robert I got Mr Jenner to correct it. I think he approved.

Jimmy Got a translation 'ave 'ee?

Robert And so, in the other tongue: Almighty and merciful God, who didst show us by the sacrifice of Thine only Son the way to victory over sin and the grave, we heartily commend to Thy keeping and care the sons of this parish who marched into the sunset in the morning of their days. Grant them with Thine Almighty hand an everlasting name and place, and victory over war   such as Thou didst gain over Death itself. This we ask in the name of Thine only Son Jesus Christ our Lord. Amen

William   A prayer for all they gone into the west...[178]

Surfing Tommies certainly drew many audiences, and the play was highly praised in both local and Britain-wide media. It is also being taught in a number of Cornish schools and colleges as a text for both GCSE and Advanced Level Drama and Theatre Studies. Several amateur companies have also performed the work outside of Cornwall, proving the story's durability. Such durability is important for Anglo-Cornish writing because it places 'Cornish narrative' onto a wider public stage, and bar a few other romantic-historical examples (*Poldark*, and the writings of Daphne du Maurier), this rarely occurs.

As the centenary of the First World War progressed, other companies saw the potential in developing drama about the conflict with a specifically Cornish agenda. One of the most spectacular of these was completed on site at the former Levant tin mine near St Just-in-Penwith from 1 to the 10 July 2016.[179] Under the direction and initiative of long-term theatre activist Jason Squibb, his company Collective Arts developed a project titled *The Trench*. For this interactive performance, the company built an entire trench in wasteland at the site, and invited audience members to become part of the narrative. Such site-specific work, of course, has several precedents in Cornwall but here the level of realism was taken to a whole new level. Audiences were required to enlist and become part of the performance itself. The National Trust supplied artefacts to help with the performance, and again, the performance was able to show the importance of Cornish engineering and mining experience in the trenches. Put alongside works such as *Surfing Tommies*, and *The Trench*, such plays were importantly demonstrating to a new generation that the Cornish had a very specific part to play in the war, and rather than being lumped in with other tommies, demonstrated that Cornish knowledge and skill could be as well used at the front-line as well as back home in mining. This was a crucial part of the success of these productions. It is significant that these creative works were being developed at the same time in which the outmoded 'British' response to the First World War was being deconstructed.[180]

In 2015-16 another play was developed by the Cornish-based theatre company North South Theatre. Not on the scale of *Surfing Tommies* or *The*

Trench, their two-hander titled *Pals* examined the relationship between two friends entering the war.[181] Although not as explicit in its depiction of Cornishness as the above two works, nonetheless *Pals* contained a vigorous response to the 'back before Christmas' agenda of politicians and recruiters (effectively individuals such as Joseph Hocking and Arthur Quiller Couch) during the conflict. Created by Jason Gerdes and Steven Kelly, the piece has toured regularly to venues in Cornwall. The two characters (George and Stan) embark on a journey which sees them moving from woeful naivety to the profound realities of war. *Pals* concludes with the poem 'For the Fallen', written by Robert Laurence Binyon (1869-1943), which appeared in *The Times* newspaper on 21 September 1914 after the Battle of Marne. The fourth stanza of the poem famously reads:

> They shall grow not old, as we that are left grow old:
> Age shall not weary them, not the years condemn,
> At the going down of the sun and in the morning
> We will remember them.[182]

These days the poem is most associated with the exhortation at memorial events conducted by the Royal British Legion, and is perhaps one of the most famous pieces of popular literature associated with the Great War. With its imagery of the 'going down of the sun' it connects well to Walling's *An Howlsedhas [The West]*. Binyon's poem further connects to Cornwall however, because it is documented that the poet composed the poem whilst sat at Pentire Point near Polzeath in North Cornwall.[183] As this volume went to press, another dramatic contribution emerged. This was *Hiraeth*, a play written by Ed Rowe and directed by Simon Harvey. The play again considered the role of miners within the conflict and their contribution to the Western Front. The drama debuted in November 2018, fittingly around the same time as the centenary of the ending of World War One. It was performed at the Wesleyan Methodist Chapel in St Just-in-Penwith, which is often labelled the 'Miners' cathedral' given its size and status. As well as this, being performed in that venue meant that it was being staged in the heart of Penwith's mining region.

That all of this theatre should emerge at this time is proof of the importance of addressing the issue of Cultural Materialism within Cornish culture. In such texts and performance, we see precisely the social reason for the production (the centenary of the beginning of the conflict), we see the political reason (in a context of wider conflicts ranging from Afghanistan and Iraq, to Syria and Yemen), the religious reason (because the war was proof perhaps of society moving in a secular direction—and that this move to secularization had, more or less been completed by the onset of the twenty-first century), and because economically, the companies knew that strategically people like to see stories couched in this time period—again, a conflict distant enough for it to be removed from reality, but also romanticised and celebrated as a 'fine' British (and hopefully Cornish) achievement. In such a way, although the wider realisation of the appalling state of conditions for the men fighting is always going to be heart-rending and emotive, here these companies were seeing the conflict (perhaps for the first time) through a purely Cornish lens. This was the appeal —whether it was innovation in staging (how does one actually stage three people surfing?) or within immersion (using the audience as the rest of one's regiment). The dramatic imperative is certainly a continuity from the past but in its take on the 'devolved' contributing territories like Cornwall, is profoundly innovative.

CONCLUSION: ANYTHING BUT NORMAL...

The success of the immediate literature around the time of the First World War, as well as more recent dramatic interpretations of Cornish experience of the conflict have proven that this war can no longer be looked at in a unionist way, and that it is now essential to consider how Cornwall, as one of the constituent parts of the British Isles, had its own individual response to the War. Because of the period the Great War took place in, contemporary writing then raises many issues of identity (often dual identity) which affected Cornish people serving a greater Britain, or more specifically 'imperial' England. The literature reflects core Cornish feeling during the conflict: the shaping of Cornish people into 'English' warriors, the reluctance of the Cornish to become involved in the conflict, the somewhat hidden place of the Cornish contribution in the Navy, their eventual Methodist sense of duty, and their understanding of the wider social and political changes that the aftermath and inter-war years brought.

The Cornu-Celtic Revival of the twentieth century had its own response to the war, but over time, has also enabled the Cornish to self-define and put themselves on the same level of performance of Celticity as other Celtic territories.[184] This redefinition has assisted and embellished the ways in which writers of the twenty-first century have dealt with identity, language, cultural memory and community in response to the conflict. As Cornwall slowly pushes for greater self-control and more community and world awareness of its language and literature, this process is unlikely to stop. Some may regard this as a cultural re-writing of history, but others will argue that it was always there anyway, located underneath a forced and imposed 'English' identity. If a constructed English identity was being shaped before and in this period, then it appears to only have been temporary, since more recent history has shown how the Cornish—to use Raymond Williams' terms—in a 'long revolution',[185] have pushed to become a 'national minority'.

Of all the texts considered, it is perhaps the novel that has been the most successful imagining of Cornish experience during the conflict, whilst autobiographical literature has helped us to understand why core Anglo-Cornish writers of the twentieth century responded to the war in certain contradictory and colliding ways. The war may have affected these writers in more ways than we perhaps ever expected. Although poetry was perhaps the least successful, we do witness the rise of publications like *An Houlsedhas [The West]* which were wholly innovative and which transgressed the usual concerns of the Cornish Revival. With the rise in the number of dramatic texts successfully depicting the Great War, it appears that Cornish literature as a whole has gone full circle. In the early twentieth century, in texts such as *Where Have You Gone Jimmy Trevenna?*, *Surfing Tommies* and *The Trench* that literature has returned to a genre which characterised writing from Cornwall for several centuries. That a conflict should stimulate this is highly interesting, and shows the capacity of Cornish drama and theatre to continually re-invent itself, and, in Kennedy's terms, once again, to provide 'useful culture'. By this he means, genuine Cornish culture that is popularly received and that is not misappropriated or invented without value or impact.[186]

This chapter has so far, avoided considering newspaper reports. It has stuck firmly to literary, theatrical and folkloric responses to the conflict. For the most part, I have left the deciphering of newspaper reports to historians and sociologists. However, one piece of writing I did find significant was a report about 'Delabole in 1915' found in the *Western Morning News*, dated 6 January 1916. The piece captures the reality of living during the conflict, and how the war dramatically affected communities—perhaps in a similar way to Rowse's reflections on Tregonissey and imagined constructions in the writings of Hocking and Quiller Couch. The picture being constructed here is of a village in North Cornwall with the war making the place 'anything but normal'. This article has sometimes looked at grand themes and issues provoking responses in literature but here are the individual effects on working-class life:

> Delabole has been anything but normal. Neither recruiting meetings nor a route march showed any immediate results, yet out of a population of 1,258, 152 are with the colours. Work at the slate quarries has been better than could have been anticipated, although only about 200 now employed instead of 500 before the outbreak of war. Although on two occasions 50 men were discharged, the management succeeded in keeping the others employed for five days a week. No new houses have been erected. Two in course of erection for a considerable time are still incomplete. It is stated that only one eligible young man in the place has not been attested. The hay harvest was a wet one, and there were but

few good ricks. The corn harvest, a late one, was a very good one, both in crop and opportunity for saving. A few men in the place are employed on relief work. Up to the present fate has favoured those who have enlisted for the war. None as yet, have been reported killed, but two young men have died from disease.[187]

This is not literature *per se*, but it is a realistic portrait of one community going through the war. Fortunately, it seems not to have suffered any losses in those who have enlisted (bar the pair killed by disease), but we know that this will shortly change. Reading such a report, one may, of course, contentiously argue that much of the literature discussed above does not really matter. A more profound script may be read on those war memorials found in almost every Cornish town and village:[188] this writing being the extraordinarily dramatic and poetic list of the names of the fallen Cornish.

NOTES AND REFERENCES

[1] I would like to thank Andrew C. Symons, Tim Saunders, Melanie James, Cedric Appleby, John C. C. Probert, Derek R. Williams, Jory Bennett, Steven Kelly, Laurence Green, Angela Broome of the Courtney Library, Royal Institution of Cornwall, Truro, and Kim Cooper and the staff of the Cornish Studies Library, Cornwall Centre, Redruth for their assistance in helping with the research for this article.

[2] Several examples may be found in Alan M. Kent, *Celtic Cornwall: Nation, Tradition, Invention,* Halsgrove, Wellington, 2014. Compare with originals in Andrew Langdon, *Stone Crosses in West Penwith,* Federation of Old Cornwall Societies, Cornwall, n.d; *Stone Crosses in North Cornwall,* Federation of Old Cornwall Societies, Cornwall, 1996. One might go further and argue that such memorials are an even older tradition. See Craig Weatherhill, *Cornovia: Ancient Sites of Cornwall and Scilly,* Alison Hodge, Penzance, 1985.

[3] See Alan M. Kent and Danny L.J. Merrifield, *The Book of Probus: Cornwall's Garden Parish,* Halsgrove, Wellington, Tiverton, 2004, p. 18.

[4] See Edward Wyrall, *The History of the Duke of Cornwall's Light Infantry, 1914-1919,* Methuen, London, 1932; Hugo White, *The Duke of Cornwall's Light Infantry,* Tempus, Stroud, 2000.

[5] See, for example, Derek R. Williams (ed.), *Henry and Katharine Jenner: A Celebration of Cornwall's Culture, Language and Identity,* Francis Boutle Publishers, London, 2007; Hugh Miners and Treve Crago, *Tolzethan: The Life and Times of Joseph Hambley Rowe,* Gorseth Kernow, Cornwall, 2002.

[6] For a context see Michael Hechter, *Internal Colonialism: The Celtic Fringe in the British national development, 1536-1969,* Routledge and Kegan Paul, London and

Henley, 1975; Hywel Dix, *After Raymond Williams: Cultural Materialism and the Break-Up of Britain,* University of Wales Press, Cardiff, 2006.

[7] See Patrick Pearse, *The Coming Revolution: The Political Writings and Speeches of Patrick Pearse,* Mercier Press, Dublin, 2012.

[8] See Matthew George Walter (ed.), *The Penguin Book of First World War Poetry,* Penguin, London, 2006. It is perhaps worth noting that several of the most famous of the First World War poets were Welsh or partly Welsh (David Jones, Edward Thomas, Wilfred Owen), partly Irish (Robert Graves) or Jewish (Siegfried Sassoon, Isaac Rosenburg).

[9] See Tim Kendall (ed.), *The Oxford Handbook of English and Irish War Poetry,* Oxford University Press, Oxford, 2007.

[10] See Paul Turner (dir.), *Hedd Wyn,* S4C, Cardiff, 1992; Jim O'Brien (dir.), *The Monocled Mutineer,* BBC One, London, 1986; David Evans, Richard Clark, Thaddeus O'Sullivan (dirs.), *The Crimson Field,* BBC One, London, 2014; Richard Boden (dir.), *Blackadder Goes Forth,* BBC One, 1989.

[11] Vera Brittain, *Testament of Youth,* Virago, London, 2014 [1933]; Pat Barker, *Regeneration,* Penguin, London, 2005 [1991-1995]; Sebastian Faulks, *Birdsong,* Vintage, London, 2014 [1993].

[12] Mark Rawlinson (ed.), *First World War Plays,* Bloomsbury, London, 2014

[13] For these debates see Brian Murdoch, *Cornish Literature,* D.S. Brewer, Cambridge, 1993; Alan M. Kent, *The Literature of Cornwall: Continuity, Identity, Difference,* Redcliffe, Bristol, 2000.

[14] See Andrew Lambert, *The Crimean War: British Grand Strategy against Russia 1853-1856,* Routledge, London, 2011; Richard R. Dawe, *Cornish Pioneers in South Africa: Gold and Diamonds, Copper and Blood,* Cornish Hillside Publications, St Austell, 1998.

[15] For a history see Thomas Shaw, *A History of Cornish Methodism,* D. Bradford Barton, Truro, 1967.

[16] Alan M. Kent, *The Theatre of Cornwall: Space, Place, Performance,* Redcliffe, Bristol, 2010.

[17] Alan M. Kent (ed.), *Voices from West Barbary: An Anthology of Anglo-Cornish Poetry 1549-1928,* Francis Boutle Publishers, London, 2000, (ed.), *The Dreamt Sea: An Anthology of Anglo-Cornish Poetry 1928-2004,* Francis Boutle Publishers, London, 2004.

[18] Tim Saunders (ed.), *The Wheel: An Anthology of Modern Poetry in Cornish 1850-1980,* Francis Boutle Publishers, London, 1999, (ed.), *Nothing Broken: Recent Poetry in Cornish,* Francis Boutle Publishers, London, 2006.

[19] Harry Patch and Richard van Emden, *The Last Fighting Tommy: The Life of Harry Patch, Last Veteran of the Trenches 1898-2009,* Bloomsbury, London, 2014. ,

[20] Michael Morpungo, *War Horse,* Kaye and Ward, London, 1982.

[21] Christopher Hampton, *The Ideology of the Text,* Open University Press, Milton Keynes, 1990.

[22] Kent, op.cit., 2000; Alan M. Kent, 'Mending the Gap in the Medieval, the Modern and the Post-Modern in New Cornish Studies; "Celtic" Materialism and the potential of presentism' in Philip Payton (ed.), *Cornish Studies: Twenty,* University of Exeter Press, Exeter, 2012, pp. 13-31.

[23] New Cornish Studies is using aspects of this methodology. See Bernard Deacon, *Cornwall's First Golden Age: From Arthur to the Normans,* Francis Boutle Publishers, London, 2016; Neil Kennedy, *Cornish Solidarity: Using Culture to Strengthen Cornish Communities,* Evertype, Portlaoise, 2016.

[24] John Terraine, *The First World War 1914-18,* Macmillan, Basingstoke, 1984; John Turner, *Britain and the First World War,* Routledge, London and New York, 1988; Brian Bond (ed.), *The First World War and British Military History,* Oxford University Press, Oxford, 1991.

[25] Adrian Gregory, *The Last Great War: British Society and the First World War,* Cambridge University Press, Cambridge, 2008; Catriona Pennell, *A Kingdom United: Popular Responses to the Outbreak of the First World War in Britain and Ireland,* Oxford University Press, Oxford, 2017.

[26] Robin Barlow, *Wales and World War One,* Gomer Press, Llandysul, 2014; Caroline Smith, *Isle of Man in the Great War,* Pen and Sword Military, Barnsley, 2015; Richard S. Grayson, *Belfast Boys: How Unionists and Nationalists Fought and Died Together in the First World War,* Continuum, London, 2010; Gavin Hughes, *Fighting Irish: The Irish Regiments in the First World War,* Merrion Press, Dublin, 2015; Kevin Munro, *Scotland's First World War,* Historic Scotland, Edinburgh, 2014.

[27] Philip Payton, *Regional Australia and the Great War: The Boys from Old Kio,* University of Exeter Press, Exeter, 2012; John Mathai and A. Kendall Hall, *India and the War,* Hawthorne, London, 2016; See also Philip Payton, *Australia in the Great War,* Robert Hale, London, 2015.

[28] Eric Leed, *No Man's Land: Combat and Identity in World War One,* Cambridge University Press, Cambridge, 2009.

[29] Quintin Barry, *The War in the North Sea: The Royal Navy and the Imperial German Navy 1914-1918,* Helion and Company, London, 2016.

[30] Terry Phillips, *Irish Literature and the First World War: Culture, Identity and Memory,* Peter Lang, New York and Oxford, 2015; Xu Guoqi, *China and the Great War: China's Pursuit of a New National Identity and Internationalization,* Cambridge University Press, Cambridge, 2005.

[31] The piece was titled *Blood Swept Lands and Seas of Red.* 888,246 poppies progressively filled the famous moat between 17 July and 11 November 2014. Each poppy represented a British military fatality during the war. *The Shrouds of the Somme* project was a public art installation by Robert Heard who wrapped 19,240 shrouded figures to be laid out in Northerhay gardens in Exeter to

represent the number of those who fell on the first day of the Battle of Somme. The event took place on 1 July 2016.

[32] Stuart Dalley, 'The Response in Cornwall to the Outbreak of the First World War' in Phillip Payton (ed.), *Cornish Studies: Eleven,* University of Exeter Press, Exeter, 2013, pp, 59-84.

[33] Pete London, *Cornwall and the First World War,* Truran, Truro, 2013; Nick Thornicroft, *Cornwall's Fallen: The Road to the Somme,* The History Press, Stroud, 2008.

[34] Cassandra Phillips (ed.) *Marjorie Williams: Letters from Lanledra - Cornwall 1914-1918,* Truran, Truro, 2007. See also Alison Spence, *More Than Names: Methodist Truronians Remembered from the Two World Wars,* Thistle Press, Truro, 2004; E.C.Matthews, *With the Cornwall Territorials on the Western Front,* Naval and Military Press, 2004; N.J.Thornicroft, *Remember These Men ... The War Dead: Three Cornish Villages - Tintagel, Boscastle and St Genys 1914-1919,* Thornicroft, Tintagel, 2012.

[35] See Lizbeth Goodman (ed.), *Literature and Gender,* Routledge, London, 1996.

[36] For an appreciation of this process see Raymond Williams, *The Country and the City,* Vintage, London, 2016 [1973].

[37] Kent, op.cit, 2000, pp. 70-114.

[38] See Alex Tickell (ed.), *Movements 1870-1940,* Routledge, London, 2016.

[39] For a perspective on this see Alan M. Kent and Derek R. Williams (eds.), *The Francis Boutle Book of Cornish Short Stories,* Francis Boutle Publishers, London, 2010, pp. 7-9.

[40] Brendan McMahon, *A Wreck upon the Ocean: Cornish Folklore in the Age of the Industrial Revolution,* Evertype, Portlaoise, 2015. ,

[41] See Kent, op.cit., pp. 195-238. See also Ella Westland (ed.), *Cornwall: The Cultural Construction of Place,* Patten Press and the Institute of Cornish Studies, Penzance, 1997.

[42] Kerry Powell (ed.), *The Cambridge Companion to Victorian and Edwardian Theatre.* Cambridge University Press, Cambridge, 2004.

[43] Kent, op. Cit, 2010, pp. 438-582.

[44] Peggy Pollard, *Bewnans Alysaryn,* James Lanham, St Ives, 1941.

[45] Alan M. Kent (ed.), *Charles Causley: Theatre Works,* Francis Boutle Publications, London, 2013.

[46] See *Royal Cornwall Gazette, West Briton* and *Cornwall County News* 1913-1919, Courtney Library, Royal Institution of Cornwall, Truro.

[47] See Charles Causley, *Collected Poems 1951-2000,* Picador, London, 2000.

[48] See A.L. Rowse, Lewis Rowe and Zofia Illinska in Kent, op.cit., 2004, pp. 57-8, pp. 110-11 and pp. 112-13.

[49] See John D. Jump (ed.), *Alfred Lord Tennyson: In Memoriam, Maud and Other Poems,* Everyman, London, 1984, pp. 154-55.

[50] Neil Kennedy, op.cit.

[51] Alan M. Kent, *Pulp Methodism: The Lives and Literature of Silas, Joseph and Salome Hocking,* Cornish Hillside Publications, St Austell, 2002.

[52] This was Silas Hocking, *Her Benny: A Story of Street Life,* Frederick Warne and Company, London, 1879.

[53] See Alan M. Kent, *Wives, Mothers and Sisters, Feminism, Literature and Women Writers of Cornwall,* The Jamieson Library, Penzance, 2004.

[54] See Simon Eliot, 'Books and the their readers' in Delia Da Sousa Correa (ed.), *The Nineteenth-Century Novel: Realisms,* Routledge, London, 2000, pp. 197-228.

[55] For an overview, see Philip Payton, *The Cornish Overseas.* Alexander Associates, Fowey, 1999.

[56] See Kent, op.cit., 2000, pp. 160-2.

[57] See Elizabeth Deeds Ermarth, *The English Novel in History 1840-1895,* Routledge, London, 1997.

[58] See Kent, op.cit, 2002, pp. 97-127.

[59] See Alan M. Kent, *Surfing Tommies,* Francis Boutle Publishers, London, 2009.

[60] This is a re-working of the Tristan and Yseult narrative. See Arthur Quiller Couch and Daphne du Maurier, *Castle Dor,* Arrow Books, London, 1994 [1962]. Du Maurier finished the novel after Quiller Couch's death.

[61] Cedric J. Appleby, *The Hockings and the First World War.* Unpublished paper, 2001, p. 1. For useful background here, see Cedric J. Appleby, '"Marching as to War": Cornish Methodists and the "Great War", in *Journal of the Cornish Methodist Historical Association,* No. 4, 1994, pp. 96-107.

[62] See Kent, op.cit, 2002, pp. 57-96.

[63] Joseph Hocking, *The Kaiser's Investments,* Ward, Lock and Company, London, 1920.

[64] See, for example, Joseph Hocking, *The Day of Judgement,* Cassell and Company, London, 1915, *Tommy and the Maid of Athens,* Hodder and Stoughton, London, 1917, *The Path of Glory,* Hodder and Stoughton, London, 1917, *The Sweat of Thy Brow,* Hodder and Stoughton, London, 1920. .

[65] Joseph Hocking, *All for a Scrap of Paper: A Romance of the Great War,* Hodder and Stoughton, London, 1915.

[66] Joseph Hocking, *The Curtain of Fire,* Hodder and Stoughton, London, 1916. *The Pomp of Yesterday,* Hodder and Stoughton, London, 1918.

[67] Cf. Simon Fuller (ed.), *The Poetry of War 1914-1989,* Longman, Harlow, 1990.

[68] Joseph Hocking, *Tommy: A War Story,* Hodder and Stoughton, London, 1916. See also Hocking, op.cit., 1917.

[69] Joseph Hocking, *The Pomp of Yesterday,* Hodder and Stoughton, London, 1918, p. 8.

[70] *Cornish Guardian,* 21 May 1915, p. 5. Joseph makes other observations on the conflict in the same edition. See p. 3.

[71] John C. C. Probert notes that 'Rev. Booth Coventry ... who had supported the clay strike of 1913, had better results than the Rev. Joseph Hocking's effort at his birth place, St Stephens, in 1915 where there were no recruits despite a rousing speech, and patriotic songs'. Booth Coventry was a United Methodist Minister and an Independent Labour Party supporter. See John C. C. Probert, 'Recruiting for the 1914-18 War and the 1851 Religious Census Etc', in *Journal of the Cornish Methodist Historical Association,* No. 4, 2000, p. 130.

[72] Hocking, op.cit., 1915, p. 5.

[73] See Appleby, op.cit., 2001, p. 6. This is a substantially truncated version of Appleby's argument. Michael E. Thorne produced a list of Hocking novels in the 1970s cataloguing some of their themes.

[74] For detail on this see Brenda Maddox, *A Married Man: A Life of D.H. Lawrence,* Minerva, London, 1995; Philip Payton, *D.H. Lawrence and Cornwall,* Truran, Truro, 2009. Events during this period are fictionalized in Helen Dunmore, *Zennor in Darkness,* Penguin, Harmondsworth, 1994.

[75] Bruce Steele (ed.), *D.H. Lawrence: Kangaroo,* Cambridge University Press, Cambridge, 1994 [1932].

[76] Hocking, op.cit., p. 253.

[77] Later obituaries make little of his specific wartime efforts, preferring to praise his public service instead. See Kent, op.cit, 2002.

[78] Joseph Hocking, *Andrew Boconnoc's Will: The Story of a Crisis,* Cassell and Company, London, 1926, *Bevil Granville's Handicap,* Hodder and Stoughton, London, 1926, *The Tenant of Cromlech Cottage,* Ward, Lock and Company, 1927, *Felicity Treverbyn: A Love Story,* Hodder and Stoughton, London, 1928, *Nancy Trevanion's Legacy,* Ward, Lock and Company, London, 1928, *The Secret of Trescobel,* Ward, Lock and Company, 1931.

[79] See Malcolm Chapman, *The Celts: The Construction of a Myth,* Macmillan, Basingstoke, 1992.

[80] For an overview, see F. Brittain (ed.), *Q: A Selection from the Prose and Verse of Sir Arthur Quiller Couch,* Dent, London, 1948. For Quiller Couch's ideology on Cornwall see Arthur Quiller Couch, *The Delectable Duchy,* Dent, London, 1915, *From a Cornish Window,* Cambridge University Press, London, 1928 [1906].

[81] John Hurst, 'Literature in Cornwall' in Philip Payton (ed.), *Cornwall Since the War: The Contemporary History of a European Region*, Institute of Cornish Studies and Dyllansow Truran, Redruth, 1992, pp. 291-308.

[82] The two most useful biographies are F. Brittain, *Arthur Quiller Couch: A Biographical Study,* Cambridge University Press, Cambridge, 1947 and A.L. Rowse, *Quiller Couch: A Portrait of 'Q',* Methuen, London, 1988. A new assessment and revised biography of Quiller Couch is much needed.

[83] For an assessment see Kent, op.cit. 2000, pp. 164-68. Quiller Couch's novel *Dead Man's Rock* (1887) was originally written as a 'pot-boiler' to help with the family's finances.

[84] See Frank McLynn, *Robert Louis Stevenson: A Biography,* Pimlico, London, 1994; Roger Lockhurst (ed.), *H. Rider Haggard: King Solomon's Mines,* Oxford University Press, Oxford, 2016 [1885].

[85] Arthur Quiller Couch, *Nicky-Nan: Reservist,* Dent, London, 1929 [1915]. Symons observes that the book is 'one of Quiller Couch's most tortured novels in which he explores the morality of war from a Christian point of view'. Correspondence with Andrew C. Symons, 17 January 2017.

[86] Bevil Quiller Couch's fiancé was May W. Canaan. Canaan was a significant poet of the First World War. In 1911, at the age of eighteen, she joined the Voluntary Aid Detachment, training as a nurse and eventually reaching the rank of Quartermaster. Their romance is documented in Charlotte Fyfe, *The Tears of War: The Love Story of a Young Poet and a War Hero,* Cavalier Press, Upavon, 2000,

[87] Quiller Couch, op.cit., p. 145.

[88] See Melanie James, 'An examination of the influence of pre-war imperial propaganda on the Cornish response to the declaration of war in 1914', MA dissertation, University of Birmingham, 2013.

[89] Thomas Quiller Couch, 'The Folklore of a Cornish Village' in *Notes and Queries: A Medium of Inter-Communication between Literary Men, Artists, Antiquaries, Genealogists Etc.* No. 312, 1855, p. 297.

[90] Arthur Quiller Couch, op.cit., p. 1.

[91] Ibid, pp. 2-3.

[92] Ibid, p. 56.

[93] See, for example, Arthur Quiller Couch, *The Astonishing History of Troy Town,* Anthony Mott, London, 1983 [1888]. It seems Quiller Couch's use of this name may be related to the Cornish being mythologically related to the Trojans and the fact that Cornish was sometimes labelled the 'Troyance Tongue'.

[94] Quiller Couch, op.cit., 1915, p. 119.

[95] Ibid, p. i.

[96] Ibid, p.ii. Even Quiller Couch himself later classed the novel as 'one of the bad uns', See Brittain, op.cit., 1947, p. 78.

[97] Robert Walling, *An Houlsedhas,* Lambessow Library, Truro.

[98] Cf: Jane Bakere, *The Cornish Ordinalia: A Critical Study,* University of Wales Press, Cardiff, 1980.

[99] Alan M. Kent (ed.), *Looking at the Mermaid: An Anthology of Cornish Literature,* Francis Boutle Publishers, London, 2017.

[100] Cf: Peter Berresford Ellis, *The Cornish Language and its Literature,* Routledge and Kegan Paul, London and Boston, 1974, pp. 147-76.

[101] Ann Trevenen Jenkin and Stephen Gadd (eds. and trs.), *Scryfer: Robert Victor Walling 1895-1976, Bard and Journalist,* Gorsedh Kernow and the Cornish Language Board, Cornwall, 2016, pp. 101-20.

[102] Michael Everson (ed.), *Henry Jenner: Handbook of the Cornish Language,* Evertype, Cathair na Mart, 2010.

[103] Trevenen Jenkin and Gadd, op.cit., pp. 7-100. Gadd does make some revisions of the original.

[104] The Walling family knew Taldir and holidayed at Lokireg in Finisterre, Brittany. Taldir was the bardic name of Francois Jaffrenou (1879-1956), a Breton nationalist and the founder of the modern Breton Gorsedd.

[105] See Paul Russell, *An Introduction to the Celtic Languages,* Longman, London and New York, 1995, pp. 111-32.

[106] See Tim Saunders, *'Scryfer an Mor'. A Recollection'* in Trevenen Jenkin and Gadd, op.cit. pp. 5-6.

[107] See Saunders. Op.cit., 1999.

[108] Trevenen Jenkin and Gadd, op,cit., pp. 97-8. These tanks were originally termed 'landships'. Their rhomboidal shape allowed them to cross trenches and climb parapets.

[109] Ibid.

[110] See *Eythen,* 1976-1978; *An Gannas,* 1977-2016.

[111] Trevenen Jenkin and Gadd, op.cit, pp. 99-100.

[112] Saunders, op.cit, 1999, p. 218.

[113] See arguments presented in Lenore A. Grenoble and Lindsay J. Whaley (eds.), *Saving Languages: An Introduction to Language Revitalization,* Cambridge University Press, Cambridge, 2006.

[114] Saunders, op.cit., pp.96-7.

[115] See Charles Thomas, 'Hardy and Lyonesse: Parallel Mythologies' in Melissa Hardie (ed.), *A Mere Interlude: Some Literary Visitors in Lyonesse,* Patten Press, Penzance, 1992, pp. 13-26, *Tintagel: Arthur and Archaeology,* English Heritage and Batsford, London, 1993.

[116] Amy Hale, Alan M. Kent and Tim Saunders (eds. and trans), *Inside Merlin's Cave: A Cornish Arthurian Reader 1000-2000,* Francis Boutle Publishers, London, 2000.

[117] See the way in which William Shakespeare's *Henry V* was used during the Second World War. See Laurence Olivier (dir.), *Henry V,* Two Cities Films, London, 1944.

[118] See James, op.cit.

[119] See Bernard Deacon, *Cornwall: A Concise History,* University of Cardiff Press, Cardiff, 2007, pp. 1-3.

[120] For further discussion of this dual identity see Kent, op.cit., 2000, pp. 147-94.

[121] See the general perception of identity in the texts in Alan M. Kent and Gage McKinney (eds.), *The Busy Earth: A Reader in Global Cornish Literature 1700-2000,* Cornish Hillside Publications, St Austell, 2008.

[122] See Hugh Miners, *Gorseth Kernow: The First 50 Years,* Gorseth Kernow, Penzance, 1978.

[123] James Dryden Hosken, *Shores of Lyonesse: Poems, Dramatic, Narrative and Lyrical,* Dent, London, 1928, pp. 167-8.

[124] The reasons for this dual identity are discussed in John Angarrack, *Our Future is History: Identity, Law and the Cornish Question,* Independent Academic Press, Bodmin, 2002.

[125] J.G. Jolly, *Easing the Burden: Collected Poems,* Palores, Redruth, 2010, pp. 28-29. The poems were edited by his daughter Sarah Jolly.

[126] See Piers Brendon (ed.), *Robert Stephen Hawker: Cornish Ballads and Other Poems,* Elephant Press, St Germans, 1975; Kent, op.cit. 2017. The latter is often sung within the Cornish traditional music scene.

[127] Ralph Dunstan (ed.), *Cornish Dialect and Folk Songs,* Jordan's Bookshop, Truro, 1932, pp. 8-9.

[128] Ibid. This song strongly echoes Andrew Boorde's thinking about the Cornish written in 1547. See Brian Murdoch (ed.), *The Dedalus Book of Medieval Literature: The Grin of the Gargoyle,* Dedalus, Sawtry, 1995, pp. 201-2.

[129] Ibid.

[130] See Donald R. Rawe, *Padstow Obby Oss: A Study in Folklore and Tradition,* Lodenek, Padstow, 1982, Tony Deane and Tony Shaw, *The Folklore of Cornwall,* Tempus, Stroud, 2003. Pp. 149-51. Jason Semmens, 'Guising, Ritual and Revival: The Hobby Horse in Cornwall' in *Old Cornwall,* 13, No. 6, 2005, pp. 39-46.

[131] Rawe, ibid, pp. 23-4.

[132] See Hampton, op.cit.

[133] See Richard F. Hardin, 'Archetypal Criticism' in G. Douglas Atkins and Laura morrow (eds.), *Contemporary Literary Theory,* Macmillan, London, 1989, pp. 42-59.

[134] See Hurst, op.cit., Kent, op.cit., 2000.

[135] Luke Thompson, *Clay Phoenix: A Biography of Jack Clemo,* Ally, London, 2016.

[136] Jack Clemo, *The Marriage of A Rebel: A Mystical-Erotic Quest,* Victor Gollancz, London, 1980. Thompson's biography casts further doubt upon the mysticism of this endeavour.

[137] See Jack Clemo, *Confession of a Rebel,* Chatto and Windus, London, 1975 [1949], pp. 18-22.

[138] Ibid, p. 20.

[139] Clemo's mother would be an important influence on him and his early writings. See Eveline Clemo, *I Proved Thee at the Waters: The Testimony of a Blind Writer's Mother,* Moorley's Bible and Bookshop, Ilkston, n.d. Eveline Clemo

once observed to Andrew C. Symons that Reggie Clemo was antagonistic to the call-up and 'had no quarrel with the Germans'. Symons also suggests that Clemo's issue with his father was that he dot fit the 'evangelical paradigm' and that, in fact, Eveline's view of Reggie was more nuanced. Correspondence with Andrew C. Symons, 17 January 2017.

[140] See, for example, Jack Clemo, *Wilding Graft,* Anthony Mott, London, 1983 [1948]. *Selected Poems,* Bloodaxe Books, Newcastle-upon-Tyne, 1988.

[141] See Andrew C. Symons, 'Jack Clemo's Italian Holiday' in *Journal of the Royal Institution of Cornwall,* 2000, pp. 186-96.

[142] Luke Thompson (ed.), *Jack Clemo: A Proper Mizz-Maze – Dialect Tales,* Francis Boutle Publishers, London, 2016.

[143] Richard Ollard, *A Man of Contradictions: A Life of A.L .Rowse,* Allen Lane, London, 1999; Philip Payton, *A.L. Rowse and Cornwall: A Paradoxical Patriot,* University of Exeter Press, Exeter, 2005. See also A.L. Rowse, *A Man of the Thirties,* Weidenfield and Nicolson, London, 1979.

[144] A.L. Rowse, *Tudor Cornwall,* Jonathan Cape, London, 1941. *The Expansion of Elizabethan England,* Macmillan, London, 1955.

[145] A.L. Rowse, *A Cornish Childhood,* Anthony Mott, London, 1982 [1942], p. 7.

[146] See Merv Davey, Alison Davey and Jowdy Davey, *Scoot Dances, Troyls and Tea Treats: The Cornish Dance Tradition,* Francis Boutle Publishers, London, 2009.

[147] See A.L. Rowse, *A Cornishman at Oxford,* Jonathan Cape, London, 1965.

[148] The subtext of much of Rowse's poetry is on this theme. See A.L. Rowse, *A Life: Collected Poems,* William Blackwood, Edinburgh, 1981.

[149] Rowse, op.cit., 1982, pp. 13-14.

[150] Ibid, p. 118.

[151] Ibid, pp. 118-19.

[152] Ibid, p. 188.

[153] Ibid, p. 277.

[154] For the full range see Sydney Cauveren, Sydney, *A.L. Rowse: A Bibliophile's Extensive Bibliography,* Scarecrow Press, Lanham, Maryland, 2000.

[155] Rowse, op.cit., 1981. See also A.L. Rowse, *Prompting the Age: Poems Early and Late,* Dyllansow Truran, Redruth, 1990. This collection might legitimately have some work influenced by the First World War, but a problem is that they are not grouped by date.

[156] Charles Causley, *Hands to Dance and Skylark,* Anthony Mott, London, 1979 [1951].

[157] Laurence Green, *All Cornwall Thunders at My Door: A Biography of Charles Causley,* Cornovia Press, Sheffield, 2012, pp. 4-16.

[158] Correspondence with Laurence Green, 12 January 2017. There are two photos of Charles Causley in the Charles Causley Literary Archive Special Collection at

the University of Exeter. One is of him in uniform on the occasion of his wedding in 1915 and the other is slightly earlier. It is catalogued as 'soldier, unknown' but is Driver Causley, as identified by Green.

[159] Ibid. David Jones (1895-1974), known popularly as 'Dai Greatcoat' was an influential Welsh-born modernist poet and artist. His epic poem *In Parenthesis* was published in 1937 and is about the First World War.

[160] Causley, op.cit. 2000, pp. 4-5.

[161] Anatole Le Braz, *Le Theatre Celtique,* Calmann-Levy, Paris, 1905.

[162] See Christopher Morrash, *a History of Irish Theatre 1601-2000,* Cambridge University Press, Cambridge, 2002.

[163] Will Coleman, *Plen-an Gwari: The Playing Places of Cornwall,* Goldentree Publications, St Buryan, 2015.

[164] Sandy Craig (ed.), *Dreams and Deconstructions: Alternative Theatre in Britain,* amber Lane Press, Ambergate, 1980; Baz Kershaw, *The Politics of Performance: Radical Theatre and Cultural Intervention,* Routledge, London, 1992; Kent, op.cit., 2000.

[165] The play in contained in Alan M. Kent (ed.), *Four Modern Cornish Plays,* Francis Boutle Publishers, London, 2010, pp. 93-179.

[166] Ibid.

[167] Ibid.

[168] See, for example, Rob Burton, 'A Passion to Exist: Cultural Hegemony and the Roots of Cornish Identity' in Philip Payton (ed.), *Cornish Studies: Five,* University of Exeter Press, Exeter, 1997, pp. 151-63.

[169] These are themes regularly found in the poetry and drama of Charles Causley.

[170] Such teaching was extremely rare within the school system during this phase. Jenner's *Handbook* was only ten years old. An exception was E.G. Retallack Hooper, who did teach Cornish to children at Mount Pleasant House School, Camborne. See Peter Berresford Ellis, *The Cornish Language and its Literature,* Routledge and Kegan Paul, London and Boston, 1974, pp. 150-1.

[171] Turley in Kent op.cit., 2010.

[172] Ibid.

[173] Ibid.

[174] See Kent, op.cit., 2009. For the historical perspective on tunnelling see Robert K. Johns, *Battle beneath the Trenches: the Cornish miners of 251 Tunnelling Company RE,* Pen and Sword Military Press, Barnsley, 2015. The Royal Engineers and the Duke of Cornwall's light Infantry were involved in tunnelling.

[175] See www.youtube.com/results?search_query=Surfing+Tommies. [accessed 13 January 2017].

[176] For a context here see Julian Putkowski and Julian Sykes, *Shot at Dawn: Executions in World War One by authority of the British Army Act,* ReadHowYouWant, London, 1998.

[177] Kent, op.cit., p. 71

[178] Ibid, p. 80-1.

[179]

www.youtube.com/watch?v=HaXeEqxqHzw&list=PL4ynELuzMUcW6WsYw1Kqvd
UY2YLLQ7VrG. /. [Accessed 13 January 2017].

[180] Barlow, op.cit.; Smith, op.cit.; Grayson, op.cit.; Hughes, op.cit.; Munro, op.cit.;
James, op.cit,.

[181] See www.youtube.com/watch?v=9f6zR-j8ldY [accessed 13 January 2017]

[182] *The Times,* 21 September 1914.

[183] A plaque marks the spot and was erected in 2003.

[184] See Peter Berresford Ellis, *The Celtic Dawn: A History of Pan-Celticism,*
Constable, London, 1993; Amy Hale, 'Performing Celtic Identities in Cornwall',
PhD thesis, University of California, Los Angeles, 1998.

[185] See Raymond Williams, *The Long Revolution,* Penguin, London, 1961. The
Cornish response can be seen in John Angarrack, *Breaking the Chains:
Propaganda, Censorship, Deception and the Manipulation of Public Opinion in
Cornwall,* Stannary Publications, Camborne, 1999 and the Facebook Group,
Kernow Matters to Us.

[186] Kennedy, op.cit,.

[187] 'Delabole in 1915' from *Western Morning News* 6 January 1916. Cf the
experiences here with that of Thomas or 'Tommy' Charles Reginald Agar-
Robartes (1880-1915) who heralded from Lanhydrock House and was heir to the
estate. He was killed at the battle of Loos in France, trying to rescue a colleague
from no-man's land.

[188] See www.cornwallswarhistory.co.uk/maps/war-memorials-2/ [accessed 13
January 2017]; Stephen Coleman, *Where Cornish Warriors Lie: Advent to Antony
Village Hall*, Vol. 1, Amazon: Kindle edition, 2016.

'SWEET ROSA TRETHOWAN OF FAIR CONSTANTINE': A CORNISH POEM OF THE GREAT WAR

Philip Payton

INTRODUCTION

Jon Stallworthy in his *Oxford Book of War Poetry* reminds us that the average 'British soldier tended to look at the [First World War] through literary spectacles'.[1] In addition to the classically-educated minority who sought solace in Virgil, Horace or Homer, there were thousands of others who found Arthur Quiller-Couch's *Oxford Book of English Verse* a comforting companion in the trenches or the barrack room. Moreover, according to Roy Strong, the sentimental and idyllic vision of a rural Britain, with its serene and timeless villages, was an imagination that inspired countless exiled British soldiers, and for which 'they fought in both world wars'. As Strong observes, this was an idyll that 'contains little that is aggressive or chauvinistic; while it is of course patriotic, it is also peaceful, romantic and tranquil'.[2] There were, of course, a great many soldiers in the Great War who turned to poetry to express their own, deeply-held feelings about the conflict and its terrors, and the more famous examples remain household names a century later – Sassoon, Graves, Rosenberg, Owen and others. But there were numerous others, who in the privacy of their diaries or notebooks, or perhaps in letters home, also penned such verses, only a relative few of which have ever appeared in print.

R.J. 'RECHARD JOHN' NOALL OF ST IVES

Among this latter group was R.J. [Richard John] Noall, born in St Ives in 1871, who in the Great War served as Bombardier in the Royal Garrison Artillery, which manned the heavy guns on the Western Front. After the war, 'Rechard John', as he was known to his friends, joined the St Ives Old Cornwall Society at its foundation in 1920, where he was a favourite speaker at meetings, his subjects ranging from dialect stories to 'The Press Gang in St Ives'.[3] Already well regarded as 'a lover and collector of all manner of antiquaries, from stone-age implements to old words, stories and songs', he published his dialect tales and verse in the *Western Echo* and *Old Cornwall*. As R. Morton Nance recalled:

a well-known local preacher, his words must have influenced many for good . . . None of us who heard him tell a Cornish story in his richest dialect and with such seductive music in his voice, or were inspired by his fervour in the singing the old folk-songs and 'curls', in taking part in guise-dance play, or giving the lead at Midsummer Bonfire or 'Neck' cutting ceremonies, will be likely to think of him apart from the dialect, the old customs, or the music in which he took such infectious delight.[4]

In 1929 R.J. Noall was admitted a bard of the Cornish Gorsedd in recognition of this work. In October of that year, shortly after his installation as a bard, his 'Cornish Comparisons' ('Collected and Rough-rhymed by R.J. Noall') appeared in the journal *Old Cornwall*, a list of twenty-seven Cornish sayings, including such gems as 'As cold as a quilkin [frog], or hot as a pie' and 'As plum as a want-pile [mole hill], or clammy as clay'.[5] A strict Methodist, Noall was also a humourist, and not above publishing 'Ribald Rhymes on Wesley':

John Wesley was a lucky man:
Of cheldern he had seven,
He put 'em in a dunkey-caart,
To drive 'em to – Poortleven.

Poortleven were a rugged rawd,
The dunkey knawed et well.
Et turned about the other way
And took'd 'em down to – Hayle.[6]

'Recherd John' was also a serious versifier, evidenced in his lengthy 'Loath to Go: A Cornish Dialect Recitation', with its stridently patriotic concluding stanza:

So I m'ght never laave Old Cornwall,
Nar paart from her rugged shore,
Far she's in my bones and sperret,
And I love her evermoore;
I am hers both mind and body,
And whatever good I've done
Come from out the heart of Cornwall, –
She's my mawther! I'm her son![7]

Noall's vision of Cornwall was a Celtic revivalist version of the British rural idyll sketched by Roy Strong, and was one that he had taken with him to the Great War, when, indeed, he had had to 'laave Old Cornwall' and was no doubt 'Loath to Go'. But he also betrayed his more practical bent as an artilleryman in his short story about a 'young tin-streamer who then worked a little water stamps on Bussow Moor [and who] fell in love with a farm servant girl called Betsy, later known as "Betsy Gunner"'. As Noall explained in a footnote, '"Gunner" is a nickname applied to people who are one-eyed or keep one eye shut, as if taking aim with a gun'.[8] His tale of Betsy Gunner was a sentimental one, and he claimed to have inherited her candle-stick holder, in the hollow stem of which he found her death certificate. He thought Betsy to have been the proudest woman in Towednack parish, after she and her tin-streaming husband had built their first cottage together. His was a romantic regard for the memory of Betsy Gunner, despite her unusual nickname and presumably unconventional appearance.

After R.J. Noall's death in 1944, R. Morton Nance and colleagues arranged for the publication of *Little Feathers and Stray Fancies*, which, as Morton Nance explained, was 'a collection of his verse written, most of it, before his "Old Cornwall" activities', and was the means by which Noall 'wish[ed] to be remembered by his friends'.[9] Among these earlier compositions, were several written when 'Recherd John' was stationed at Pendennis castle. But most striking was his 'Sweet Rosa Trethowan of Fair Constantine', which exhibited all the traits discussed above, from the yearning for the rural idyll of 'dear old Cornwall, fair land of mine' to the longing for 'Sweet Rosa' herself. The extent to which the poem is autobiographical is not entirely clear. It is dated 'Flanders, 1916', and finds its author recovering from a head injury in Ypres [Wipers]. Trethowan was (and is) the name of a long-established family in Constantine, although 'Rosa' appears to be fictional, perhaps to protect the innocent, as it were:

Sweet Rosa Trethowan,
If you lived at Crowan,
I'd find my way thither, on wet days or fine,
But many times nearer,
And a thousand times dearer
To me, is the parish of fair Constantine.

Chorus: – O Rosa, Sweet Rosa! I wish thee wert mine
To live with for ever;
I'd part from thee never.
Sweet Rosa Trethowan, of fair Constantine.

My heart's nearly breaking,
Each morn when awaking
The blue hills of France rise twixt thee and us fighters;
And I toss on my rude bed,
And aches my poor cracked head
In a hospital ward here in 'Wipers'.

But when the war's over,
And sailing past Dover,

I reach dear old Cornwall, that fair land of mine,
Perhaps you will meet me
And be pleased there to greet me,
On the platform, at Falmouth, near fair Constantine.

CONCLUSION

It is not great literature but it is not mere doggerel either. It is of the moment, heart-felt and sincere, and is for us an authentic insight into the emotional response of one Cornish soldier on the Western Front in the Great War. It tells us nothing startling or unexpected, and in its simple way is entirely predictable. Yet 'Sweet Rosa Trethowan of Fair Constantine' deserves to be remembered as a genuine reflection of Cornwall and the Cornish in the Great War. It can surely take its place alongside better known literary vignettes such as D.H. Lawrence's dramatic expulsion as a spy, John Betjeman's account of a Padstow soldier in the trenches on the eve of May Day, and A.L. Rowse's description of the impromptu furry dance that wended its way through the streets of St Austell when the Armistice was announced in November 1918.[10]

NOTES AND REFERENCES

[1] Jon Stallworthy, *The Oxford Book of War Poetry*, Oxford University Press, Oxford, 1984, new ed. 1995, p.xxvi.

[2] Roy Strong, *Visions of England,* The Bodley Head, London, 2011, p.147.

[3] *Old Cornwall*, Vol. lll, Summer 1940, pp.302-303.

[4] R. Morton Nance, 'Introduction', in R.J. Noall, *Little Feathers and Stray Fancies*, W.J. Jacobs, St Ives, n.d but c.1952, p5. I am indebted to Bert Biscoe for drawing my attention to this collection, many years ago.

[5] *Old Cornwall*, No.10, October 1929, p.29.

[6] *Old Cornwall*, Vol.ll, No.6, Winter 1933, p.13. Although Noall did not say so, this rhyme may have been an allegorical play on words – Poortleven rhyming with Heaven, and Hayle with Hell.

[7] *Old Cornwall*, Vol.II, No.II, Summer 1936, pp.17-18.

[8] *Old Cornwall*, Vol. lV, No.2, Winter 1943, pp.85-86.

[9] Noall, c.1952, p.43.

[10] Philip Payton, *D.H. Lawrence and Cornwall*, Truran, St Agnes, 2009, pp.38-42; Philip Payton, *John Betjeman and Cornwall: 'The Celebrated Cornish Nationalist'*, University of Exeter Press, Exeter, 2010, p.69; Philip Payton, *A.L. Rowse and Cornwall: A Paradoxical Patriot*, University of Exeter Press, Exeter, 2005, paperback edition 2007, p.59.

INVESTIGATING THE BLAMELESS IN THE ECONOMIC CONTEXT OF POST-WAR ST JUST: LOOKING BACK AT THE 1919 LEVANT MINE INCIDENT

Victoria Jenner

INTRODUCTION

In the year following the Armistice Cornwall suffered a dilapidating loss to its mining community in St. Just – both literally and figuratively. Widely publicised as 'The Levant Mining Disaster of 1919' and close to four months after the Treaty of Versailles was signed in June 1919, 31 miners from the age of 18 through to 61 years old were killed during a shift change. It involved the deaths of at least five men who fought in the war: Henry Andrews, Matthew Eddy Matthews, James Henry Oats, Leonard Semmens, and Vingoe Trembath. From what can be ascertained from those 19 injured, at least two were also survivors of the trenches, Charlie Freestone and Sidney Dennis.[1] The proximity of the Great War influences how contemporary media marks this event as a haunting affair in 'British' mining history, ultimately feeding twentieth century curation of the Levant Mine event as a sad mishap that must not be overlooked for its demonstration of heroism and Cornish martyrdom.[2] Yet ironically details of the event and how it was handled fall victim to negligence and misrepresentation of the time, ultimately distracting from the most significant question that has not yet been answered – what really caused the demise of the Levant Mine?

The confusion around the circumstances of Monday 20 October 1919 also raises another query, into whether journalistic enquiry around the disaster was transparently regurgitated. This becomes apparent today, in an age where curatorial interpretation strives for systematic reliability, and leaves the public recognising the Levant Mine as a site of conflicted narratives. On one hand it is represented as a site commemorating the 31 lives lost, on the other it celebrates the economic affluence of Cornish mining up to this event. Both are true and hold vigour in their own right, yet when presented simultaneously, can be received as condemning the 'disaster' as the catalyst for the dissolution of Cornish mining and thus slightly insensitive to those lost lives. However, this subconscious condemnation felt today about the Levant mine incident is not entirely misplaced. The seed of conspiracy is sewn when reflecting on contemporary coverage that sensationalises the miners as heroic characters, much akin to the style of literature that was published during war-time. There is an undeniable sense that the public is being fed an alternate version of the truth – an enhanced 'bed-time story' that will conceal the crippling economy, the already nervous shareholders, the poorly sustained mining equipment, the disgruntled miners who are striking for higher pay and better working conditions. The media turns the '1919 disaster' into an international bid to raise funds for the bereaved, and does so by riveting readers with horror, agony and heartfelt revivals of war-time heroism. However, by doing this, the media also marks Levant as a deteriorating point for British mining activity. The contemporary editor of the *Mining Magazine*, Edward Walker, explicitly declares '[t]he accident at Levant was the worst disaster yet experienced at an English non-ferrous metal mine since the flooding of East Wheal Rose in 1846'[3]. Now the mine itself is memorable for the infliction of unjustness on the lives of local people who had just returned to normalise the mining economy, to continue and better the British industrial economy after a dark, turbulent period. The power of the journalistic voice in this instance is ultimately catastrophic and can be argued as ultimately handing the Levant Mine its own death warrant in 1930. As the official published reports into the health and safety of the issue is limited, and conducted by Boydell, the Inspector of the time, the media coverage is hence integral to the historic inquiry into what happened, safeguarding the only surviving interview records with the miners themselves.

HISTORICAL BACKGROUND

Figure 1 - A contemporary image taken of 'Men wait[ing] for news on the day after the disaster' for a local newspaper. The headline declares 'THRILLING STORIES OF RESCUE AND ESCAPE'.[4]

The Levant Mine incident became represented and known as the 'worst disaster in Cornish mining history' but it was meant to be a model of innovation back in the nineteenth century.[5] First, what is a man engine? The mine's man engine functioned as an elevator, with the aim to reduce the waste of workers' energy that would be spent on laborious ladder climbing from level to level. Instead, the man engine would take the men up and down the shaft, saving valuable resources for the company. By 1855 Levant's levels had increased to 1380 feet below adit (the mine's entrance) and roughly 1600 feet deep from the earth's surface. Thus, '[t]he agents having recommended that a man engine be erected on Phillips Shaft: Resolved that the necessary steps be taken for carrying out the same at once'.[6] Bearing in mind, contemporary mining professionals fully supported the man engine as the safest option of appliance to implement into the mine. For instance, the *Mining and Smelting Magazine* debates 'the various appliances' that can upgrade the use of the ladders with technology. Just a few years after Levant's man engine construction it was noted that 'In Cornwall there is a large party who object to the use of the skip, or any other similar appliance, in the raising of men, principally on the ground of its being dangerous, and who believe that the man-engine is the only machine properly applicable in the varyingly inclined shafts of metallic mines'.[7]

The innovation of the man engine can be emphasised as even more exciting for The Levant Mine Company and especially William Thomas and James Henry Edwards, the man engine drivers, when it was completed by April 1857 and driven for the first time three months later. Nevertheless, the rapid implementation of the man engine prior to industrial debate and testing, could be another long-term aspect relating to Levant's downfall. The engineer's notes demonstrate that the appliance was not erected on Phillips Shaft as the agents had recommended, but instead on Daubuz's Shaft, where the 1919 collapse takes place. Despite other professionals arguing for the safety and efficiency of the man engine years later, the original style implemented into Cornish mining in the middle of the nineteenth century could be called a brash move that dismissed safety measures as futile and chose a more successful shaft for corporate gain.

THE INCIDENT OF 1919

A source described what occurred in a newspaper article published nine days later:

> When the man engine ascends and is at the top of the stroke as on Monday (the men having completed their day's work about 2.30pm), the machine was practically full of men, each one, as it were standing above the head of the other on the projecting step. An instant later all these miners would have stepped off and paused on the side platforms, or sollors, for the next up lift of the engine. That instant meant life or death to thirty or more men. The scene was indescribable. The rod released from its top cracked in several places, and the structure crashed down in a mass of debris. As its foot was at the bottom of the shaft it could only have dropped the twelve feet if it had not snapped in other places. The worst chokage was in the upper part of the shaft'.[8]

The same article provides an information disclaimer at the end of the article, stating '[t]he full tale has not yet been told; but we give our readers the tragic story as it has been gleaned by our staff'.[9] The newspaper documents 'the tragic story' of the survivors yet overlooks family members and any negative formulation of emotion that could make the story seem non-heroic. This seems like an atypical approach to war-time literature, an element that will be discussed. The overall significance of these media

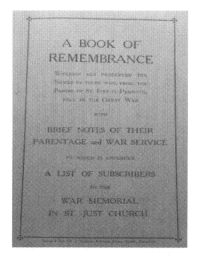
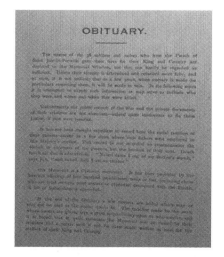

Figure 2 - The only insight into how the community responded is represented through physical manifestations of commemoration, for the War and then for the 1919 mine collapse. Here shows a stained-glass window [centre] and The Book of Remembrance [left], including an obituary [right] in the local church, St. Just, Penwith. The obituary states 'this memorial is a Christian memorial' and that 400 parishioners contributed towards its construction.[10] These visual embodiments reveal the community's technique of memorialisation for the 38 locals who 'gave their lives for King and country' in the Great War.[11]

portrayals were the repeated motif of the faulty appliance being an 'accident'. No blame, feelings of unjustness, or accusation, were at all demonstrated in news and magazine reports. This is what underlines the whole incident as slightly odd, when a modern-day reader attempts to realise the overwhelming amounts of grief that must be manifesting around the local community at this time.

With Cornwall responding to the backlash of reduced government funding, it is also hard to ignore what must have been felt during this time when warfare and the mine disaster had broken apart so much of the community. At the inquest, the verdict of the Jury was 'accidental death' caused by a defective part of the metal, relating to the cap which appeared

Figure 3 - The memorial plaque to the men who lost their lives in the Levant Man Engine Disaster of 20 October 1919.[12]

corroded. Hence, 'metal fatigue' was the criminal in this instance. Yet inquiries into how this happened and why this developed cannot be accounted for. The Levant Mine Company continued to maintain the mine after the incident. They demonstrated hope that the mine can be 'rejuvenated' in the months prior to a further four deaths in 1920, and still no condemnation is officially pointed their way, unless one includes Edward Walker's side remark (the editor of the *Mining Magazine* at the time). Is it fair to ask whether a cultural desensitization to death and a national socio-economic exhaustion allowed the overlooking of the mechanical error verdict? Was it simply accepted as a mere unfortunate by-product of a country crippled from the Great War? Or was the verdict lacking as not all bases were covered? These are questions that are present in the following discussion, when exploring how the media and the official inquisition into the 'Levant Mine disaster of 1919' were driven by an atypical post war behaviour that sought to keep spirits high, albeit relinquishing the quest for accountability.

QUESTIONING ACCOUNTABILITY

The accountability of the faulty man engine has been up to now the most apparent cause of the disaster, collapsing the shaft and in turn, firmly condemning mechanical error as being the prime culpable cause behind these deaths. The man engine, to provide a definitive overview, was a steam-driven system that was utilised for the sole purpose of transporting the miners vertically up and down the shaft, allowing them to mount the many levels. Yet the economic, social and political realities were a compelling force upon the mining industry during 1919, and can be, in turn, equally incriminated as the guilty parties. Britain incurred 715,000 military deaths (with more than twice that number wounded), the destruction of 3.6% of its human capital, 10% of its domestic and 24% of its overseas assets, and spent well over 25% of its GDP on the war effort between 1915 and 1918.[13] Yet that was far from the sum of the losses that the Great War inflicted on the British economy; economic damage continued to accumulate throughout the 1920s and beyond.[14] Two economic historians, Findlay and O'Rourke, describe 'World War I [as bringing about] the liberal economic order of the late 19th century to an abrupt halt' and suggesting that Britain in turn was replaced with countries such as Japan and the United States, in the international markets.[15] As the British economy began to react to a consistent loss of world market share, exports generated from Cornwall in the mid-1920s mirrored 75% of its 1913 output, ultimately enforcing financial restrictions upon The Levant Mine Company, forcing high levels of unemployment and an operational negligence.[16]

The production of Cornwall's mined materials had been increasingly generated under high intensity during the years Britain had been involved with the international conflict, and as a result, suffered physical neglect from government funds, leading to deteriorated, exhausted conditions in the mines themselves.[17] As Nicholas Craft suggests, the backdrop to Britain's continued 'weak productivity performance' led to 'a number of new problems emerg[ing] from a transition of peace that was fraught with difficulty'.[18] The policy choices made after the war implicated a 'big squeeze' to preserve fiscal sustainability and thus the expected social pressure to maintain a rigorous churning out of copper and tin. By the time that Armistice and peace arrived, the British economy was in such a state of disrepair that funds could not be allocated for the upkeep of technical materials but instead concentrated 81% of the overall government expenditure on the revival of the British militia and its defence.[19] Instead, 1% was spent on Health and Safety, accompanied by a 1% welfare spending cut - a palpable representation of how government values were placed into the production of materials over safety within the workforce. That said, the country was financially waning and incurring debts up to 136% of its gross national product.[20] When placing this into an everyday context, the ordinary working man was expected to continue working to produce high standard products, with minimalist pay.

Looking at Levant Mine from an economic perspective, it would have been overly strenuous financially to replace the beam's man rod, especially as when this was a bespoke aspect of the equipment, installed in 1857 and the last design being actively used in local mining. A month after the incident, an anonymous 'Cambourne Correspondent' even divulges '[t]his particular man-engine appears to have been installed some 70 years ago, and has been in continuous use ever since'.[21] Not directly in response to the anonymous commentator yet with similar intent, the editor Walker again comments '[i]t is desirable to remind readers that serious accidents also occur with the most up-to-date winding appliances, and that, in any case, the blame for the delay in reorganizing the mining methods at Levant does not rest on the management but with the owners of the mineral rights'.[22] Here it is interesting that Walker places sympathy with the manager, who would have been Major Freethy Oats and supposedly closer hence more knowledgeable about the mechanistic workings of the man engine. Yet this immediately underlines contemporary judgements surrounding the hierarchical system of responsibility as in fact Oats had only been manager since his father's death, just over a year prior to the incident. Walker instead points the finger at The Levant Mining Company as negligent on reviewing their own mining methods, blaming their inability to upgrade the man engine. The blame game is here problematic, as Oats' inexperience could be accounted, yet at the same time, the Inspector concludes that '[the man engine] has been regularly inspected and the materials renewed at various times'.[23] Plus it is significant to recognise the contemporary attitudes towards the man engine. Instead of wasting valuable energy through the climbing of ladders which equally brings their own set of dangers, the man engine would have been a welcome piece of equipment by the miners themselves, preventing them from needing to access the levels in a considerably anarchic fashion. However, when looking through records of the inquisition, combined with media coverage, the consideration that the blame could be placed upon individuals has been entirely disregarded.

The concept or inquiry into the possibility of human error appears entirely absent. Ideas behind why the rod may have broken were immediately sentenced to mechanical error, deflecting entirely the possibility of bad managerial judgement or a percentage of the workforce suffering from post-traumatic stress disorder. The concept of placing a group of former soldiers into claustrophobic spaces was not even explored as being a liable cause, and thus evidence of the miners' psychological states before and after the incident were not recorded unless officially committed to Bodmin Asylum.[24] Scientific enquiry into certain mental health disorders caused by war-time experiences were battling the early stages of gaining recognition as a serious condition, and seem most likely not even a consideration for the Inspector. Responses to the disaster had to be taken on a personal and individual basis. For instance, one victim of the incident was Thomas Murley who fought as a Sergeant, 1st Battalion DCLI from the end of 1916 to 1918 in France.[25] According to the 1911 Census, Thomas was married to Theresa Jane Oats, widowing her at age 50 with four children when killed at Levant.[26] After his death in 1919, Theresa remarries, suggesting a requirement to support a family that was in need of the financial aid that was not being provided by the Relief Fund. Was it the lack of financial aid that was not provided by the government in support of the families, highlighting remarriage as a possible form of financial desperation in a little mining village? The widow was probably fortunate considering the low levels of compensation to have been able to remarry which may have brought essential financial benefits.

MEDIA COVERAGE

Language is integral to looking back at how Levant mine was presented and received by the public. Written records of those directly involved on the day of the 'disaster' are sparse and when found, problematic. Contemporary newspaper accounts of the incident provide quoted insights into what occurred within the mine shaft yet taking these quotes as the said truth is undeniably dubious and thus drive our modern-day investigations along a rather precarious line of enquiry. Many first-hand accounts have been adopted by contemporary journalists, providing articulate portrayals of heroism and martyrdom. Then there is the common motif that the man engine fails by 'accident'.[27] Note how 'accident' has automatically generated a sense of blamelessness, that the 'disaster' has not yet been held to account. The language used in the media after the Levant Mine deaths could be dripping with a subconscious political agenda to maintain a controlled serenity around the disaster – distracting the public from the economic decline surrounding Cornish mining. This following examination deconstructs the most accessible evidence 'left behind' after the Levant Mine incident, how the event has since been treated and whether this treatment can give us a modern-day perspective of culpability. Another aspect of media interest was the intention of raising as much money as possible for the Miners Relief Fund. For this to be successful the Cornish miners had to be presented as a new post war generation of heroes concocted for the diasporic communities abroad.

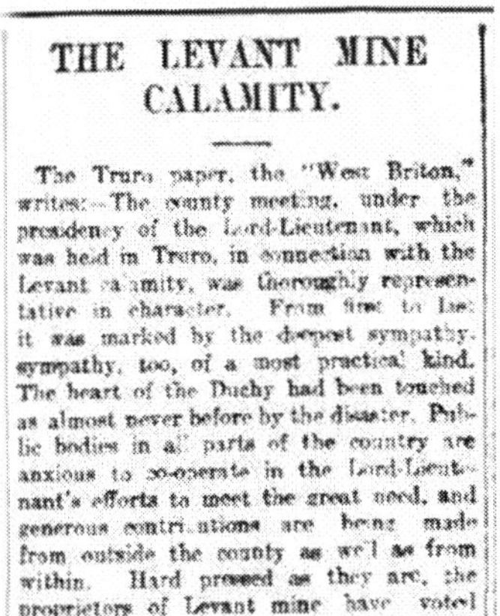

THE LEVANT MINE CALAMITY.

The Truro paper, the "West Briton," writes:—The county meeting, under the presidency of the Lord-Lieutenant, which was held in Truro, in connection with the Levant calamity, was thoroughly representative in character. From first to last it was marked by the deepest sympathy. sympathy, too, of a most practical kind. The heart of the Duchy had been touched as almost never before by the disaster. Public bodies in all parts of the country are anxious to co-operate in the Lord-Lieutenant's efforts to meet the great need, and generous contributions are being made from outside the county as well as from within. Hard pressed as they are, the proprietors of Levant mine have voted £1,000 to the County Relief Fund, while the Dockers' Union are displaying an eager generosity in the great cause. In seconding a resolution of condolence with the sufferers proposed at a meeting of the Cornish Institute of Engineers, Mr. M. T. Taylor, of East Pool and Agar, expressed his appreciation of, and admiration for,

Figure 4 - This newspaper article was published in Adelaide in 1919, and adopts 'The Truro Paper's' sensationalism of the 'calamity'. It states, 'the heart of the Duchy had been touched as almost never before by the disaster' encouraging an abundance of financial aid from international and British communities to help the bereaving families.[28]

By tactfully denoting the names of the 'generous givers' alongside their rising amounts, the fund is well marketed with stories of the brave and then the impoverished, lonely families that have been left behind. The sensational marketing continues and leaps from the paper onto the screen. Langford Lovell Price's words: '[t]here is no county in England with a stronger individuality than Cornwall'[29] become the introductory words for a 38 second government feature film that appealed nationally and internationally for money and support. Whilst watching 'Shots of the Broken shaft at the Levant Tin Mine', the viewer saw the remnants of a nightmare - angles of the broken shaft and the disorientated, confused and shaken survivors. The feature headlines the disaster like a Hollywood feature film with sombre music playing and 'St Just. - Cornish Mine Disaster - The broken shaft at the Levant Tin Mine that fell causing heavy death-roll'.[30] Evidently the intention of the broadcast was to emotively engage the international and national public with the disaster in a plight to better fundraise. By demonstrating scenes of chaos and death, the Great War was again replayed within the minds of the surviving public. So, if war revival imagery was being used for the fundraising effort, then why did this not extend to drawing from the County War Fund to aid the crisis? As mentioned before, a proportion of the miners killed and injured had officially fought in the First World War. The others had either continued the output of tin and copper throughout the war, which ultimately went towards the production of warfare machinery and weaponry. As the Council found it necessary to prevent the families, widowers and injured miners/ex-soldiers initiates to benefit from the county war fund after the Levant crisis, it highlights how they viewed the collapse of the man engine as entirely detached from the war. The very fine boundary lines of who could draw from the fund did not, in this instance, include the families of the surviving soldiers who were now killed from the mechanical error. Nor was the man engine failure considered a result of poor mining methods induced by the war-time economy. The simple act of refusing the use of the war fund was then outlined through the media practice of fundraising for a separate benevolence fund for the crisis.

During a conversation interview in 1919, Sir Robert Horne, Minister of Labour between 1919 and 1920, and President of the Board of Trade between 1920 and 1921, was asked his opinion in relation to government funds going towards the victims of various mining disasters. Horne answered:

> I have been asked to reply to this question. I am aware of the temporary stoppage of work at Pendeen in consequence of the tin-mining disaster, and every effort is being made to place those men who are willing to take work temporarily in other districts. The National Relief Fund is only designed

to assist cases of distress arising out of the War, and would, I fear, not be available for the purpose suggested. I do not know of any funds which cover such. In the past they have usually been met by local relief funds and fortuitous occurrences.[31]

Horne's answer further substantiates the economic depravity that was extending far and wide to affect not only British international exports but also the micro-scale of the relief fund. The eligibility for the fund could only be stressed as a 'war-related' loss, despite many of the miners being former 'patriots' or had arguably suffered due to the war sapping financial resources away from the machinery that led to their misfortune. It is again not so surprising to then perceive the strikes against low wages for the mining community as expressions of grievance upon the lack of financial support provided during the disasters caused by mechanical faults. When considering the three-month lockdown that Levant mine underwent between 1918 to 1919, it would not be a far leap to consider this as an act of defiance against a government that appeared 'unsympathetic and ungrateful' during a period of rehabilitation for the miners who survived the war.[32] Many of the men who returned to the mines were stationed with the tunnelling division, leaving the maintenance of the domestic mines with the elderly and young boys. Although it would be unjustified to overlook the economic restraints Britain faced as a nation, it does not erode the current viewpoint that those grievances expressed by the Cornish mining communities were seemingly dismissed during a period when one of their central industrial activities was at threat of dwindling away.

LEVANT AS AN ENDURING SPACE

Although one would assume the continuity of the mine with assured and renewed safety procedures would be a moral requirement for the company, this was not the case. The engineer's report states, 'it will be necessary to sink a new shaft and provide new equipment, but meanwhile the old shaft and equipment can be used to keep the mine developing and producing sufficiently'.[33] The mine then suffered yet another tragic event on 13 August 1920 '[when] four men were killed down the mine by a mysterious blasting accident, working on the 190 level'.[34] Again, media coverage characterised the deaths as enigmatic despite the contingency report published by Major Oats six months earlier that indicated the continual use of old materials and the old shaft until 'this new mine can be rejuvenated'.[35] The shortage of male labour became a 'massive hindrance upon the mine', limiting the ore raised 'and effectively seal[ing] off the bottom of the mine with its untold riches', that essentially led to its unsustainability.[36] As a result of both disasters, the mine and its workers were under strain. Already the lack of the man engine meant the regressing back to manually moving up and down the top 150 fathoms using ladders, likening working conditions to the 'dark ages'.[37] This continued restricted access reflected the emerging economic strain of Levant Mine Ltd, intensifying when enforced redundancies became the beginning of the end for St Just's active mining community.[38] By the 1930s, the required amount to keep Levant afloat would have been an additional £120,000 of investors' funds - a figure that was heightened as metal prices declined in Britain.[39] This reduced state was a much different story to Britain's once leading economic position prior to the Great War, with the possession of 27% of the world's manufactured exports and holding a much higher share of trade in GDP (54%) than other leading economies such as Germany (40%) and the United States (10%).[40]

Many repercussions of the Great War could be to blame for the demise of the Cornish mining economy: whether that be a lack of skilled men, the absence of public funding or a resulting ideology to overlook problematic company procedures. Many variables contributed towards the decline of such a prominent aspect of the Cornish identity but the Levant mine adopts a microcosmic-like status for the whole of the British export status, demonstrating how the years during the Great War weakened its once prolific presence. The Levant Mine incident embodies the problematic and turbulent realities that local people faced when returning into a post-war period. Although society rejoiced at the end of the conflict, other barriers arose, and Britain was forced to adapt to its new economic position as a struggling competitor in the international field of export. In conjunction to this macro picture it was the everyday person who was impacted. This being either via finance – reacting to lower wages and a different standard of living, or whether it be through what the St Just mining community reflects – a further loss of life leading to the gradual forfeiture of a local livelihood. Yet the mining disaster appears not only as a catalyst but a turning point for Cornish identity. Roger Bryant, a present-day composer, underlines the initial sense of anxiety surrounding the loss of such an economic-centred identity for Cornwall with 'Cornish Lads'. The song asks: 'Cornish lads are fishermen and Cornish lads are miners too. But when the fish and tin are gone, what are the Cornish boys to do?'[41] The answer to Bryant's question was confronted by twentieth century writers like Daphne Du Maurier, who recognised Cornwall as instead a historic landscape to be celebrated for a once vibrant source of British trade and power. Today, Levant appears as the essential centre and singularly recognised landmark of the local community, and despite rendering the investigation into the cause of the disaster as hidden, obscured and overlooked, the growth of mass tourism has attracted visitors universally to the site.[42] The mining landscape is now 'imagined as [an] enduring space...

forged over millennia through sacrifice and of blood and toil... [and] believed to have been an essential part of national identity from time immemorial'.[43]

NOTES AND REFERENCES

[1] The personal details included here come from a research project in support of commemorative drama, *The Trench*, performed at Levant in July 2016. The sources for this were mostly census data, parish records, newspaper reports, military service papers and conversations with local people.

[2] Nine days after the incident, *The Cornishman and Cornish Telegraph* published an article featuring characters as 'The Plucky Miner' and 'the hero' whilst sensationalising the event with dramatic sub-titles, such as 'HOW THE ENTOMBED MINERS WERE FOUND' and 'A MARVELOUS ESCAPE'. *The Cornishman And Cornish Telegraph,* 29 October 1919.

[3] Edward Walker, *Mining Magazine*, November 1919

[4] *The Cornishman And Cornish Telegraph,* 29 October 1919.

[5] 'Cambourne Correspondent', *Mining Magazine*, November 1919

[6] The minutes of the adventurers' meeting of 14 August 1855 record.

[7] *Mining & Smelting Magazine*, June 1862

[8] *The Cornishman And Cornish Telegraph,* 29 October 1919.

[9] Ibid.

[10] 'Obituary' in The Book of Remembrance of St Just in Penwith, Penwith, 1919.

[11] Ibid.

[12] This plaque was previously in Trewellard Wesleyan Chapel and is now in the Hard Rock Museum at Geevor, photo: Clint Hosking.

[13] S. Broadberry & M. Harrison, 'The Economics of World War I: An Overview' in *The Economics of World War I,* Cambridge University Press, Cambridge, 2005, pp. 3-40.

[14] Nicholas Crafts 'Walking wounded: The British economy in the aftermath of World War I' in *New Vox Eu Column.* 2014. Web. 27. 08. 2014.

[15] Ronald Findlay & Kevin O'Rourke, *Power and Plenty,* Princeton University Press, Princeton, 2007, p. 429.

[16] S J Cochrane, 'Britain's Position in the World Economy: Increasing Returns and International Disruption, 1870-1939', unpublished D. Phil. Thesis, University of Oxford, 2009.

[17] It is equally important to realise that the man engine had been welcomed by the workers of the mine. Contemporary safety studies concluded that the use of a man engine was actually safer in practice than using long ladders as there was less danger of them falling off due to exhaustion. In the Annual Report of the Royal Institution of Cornwall for 1848, published six years after the introduction of the first man engine at the Tresavean and United Mines, looked at the frequency of accidents, the amount of disease and the facility of labour in the deeper levels of those mines since the adoption of the man engine. George A Michell, one of the

surgeons to the Tresavean and United Mines, wrote '[f]rom my observations I should say that pulmonary and cardiac diseases are certainly of less frequent occurrence in this district than before the introduction of the Man Engine, and that the miner, independent of the evil effects of climbing on the respiratory and circulatory organs, has not his strength so exhausted or his constitution so weakened as was formerly the case, and consequently his power of resisting disease is greatly increased.'

[18] Ibid.

[19] Christopher Chantrill, 'UK Public Spending Since 1900' in *UK Public Spending Statistics*. 2018. Web. 23.07.2015.

[20] Ibid.

[21] *Mining Magazine*, November 1919

[22] Ibid.

[23] *The Cornishman And Cornish Telegraph,* 29 October 1919.

[24] We can ascertain that the psychological states of the returned soldiers would have been a factor in some way. For instance, we have the Asylum records for William Henry Ellis, a tunneller in the war who returned home and was committed to the county mental asylum at Bodmin after being first on the scene of another accident at Levant when four trammers were killed in August 1920.

[25] Thiepval Memorial. St Just WM, Bolitho Club. 2014.

[26] *UK Census Online*, '1911 Census: Sergeant Thomas Murley' (2014). Web. 02.04.1911.

[27] *The Cornishman And Cornish Telegraph,* 29 October 1919.

[28] *The Cornishman And Cornish Telegraph,* 29 October 1919.

[29] Langford Lovell Price, *'West Barbary'; or Notes on the system of Work and wages in the Cornish Mines [London: 1891]*, H. Frowde, London, 2008, p. 19.

[30] *British Pathé Film Archive.* "St Just. - Cornish Mine Disaster - The broken shaft at the Levant Tin Mine that fell causing heavy death-roll." 27.10.1919. Web. 01:08:52:00

[31] *Hansard Parliament.* 'Hansard Commons'. (vol.) 123. 2018. Web. 17.12.1919. pp 402-3. https://api.parliament.uk/historic-hansard/commons/1919/dec/17/levant-mine-disaster © UK Parliament

[32] *Hansard Parliament.* 'How to Regenerate Camborne, Pool and Redruth'. 2004. 17.12.1919. Web. p193. https://api.parliament.uk/historic-hansard/commons/1919/dec/17/levant-mine-disaster © UK Parliament

[33] *Mining Magazine*, March 1920, p. 150

[34] Ibid.

[35] *Mining Magazine*, March 1920, p. 151

[36] Ibid.

[37] David J Sinclair, 'Saint Just, The Mine. St. Just Mining Area' in *Phoenix Mine Heritage,* 2009.

[38] Ibid.

[39] Noall Cyrell, 'The Peril of the '40 Backs'' in *Levant: The Mine Beneath the Sea,* D.B. Barton, Truro, 1970, p. 121.

[40] Cochrane, 'Britain's Position in the World Economy', 2009.

[41] www.songoftheisles.com/2014/04/25/cornish-lads/ [last accessed 1 December 2018].

[42] When appropriating the term 'landmark', I draw on how landscape provides locals with a solid, seemingly unchanging centre which is personally/ emotionally adopted. Communal memories of the Levant tragedy ensure that the site remains controversial as can be seen in a BBC news feature on 16 February 2017: www.bbc.co.uk/news/av/uk-england-cornwall-38998923/poldark-location-parking-charge-controversy-at-levant-mine-cornwall [last accessed 1 December 2018]

[43] Tim Edensor, *National Identity, Popular Culture and Everyday Life,* Berg, Oxford, 2002, p. 66.

'SERVED, SURVIVED AND THE SEWING OF SEEDS': HOW HELSTON REMEMBERS THE GREAT WAR

Froshie Evans

The Museum of Cornish Life in Helston is nothing short of a tardis of historical artefacts.[1] From geology to famous nineteenth century boxer Bob Fitzsimmons, this humble museum is bursting with artefacts collected and curated from the communities around West Cornwall. In recent years, however, this museum has gained national recognition for its pop-up centenary exhibitions of the Great War, known as the Helston World War One Heritage Project.[2] The woman who curated it, Mrs Martine Knight, has been doing the project as a volunteer and developed it originally with the town council, then as an independent project. Each year there has been a focus on different aspects of the Great War and its concluding exhibition this year has included aspects of the Roaring Twenties to show how the people of Helston and the surrounding parishes looked to the future for hope and peace after such dark times. The project has been funded by the National Lottery, and its success led to Knight having been invited to London for the Royal Armistice Remembrance Ceremonies, including the People's Parade in which she laid a wreath and a set of cards to represent the Helston servicemen who lost their lives in the war.[3] Perhaps the most intriguing thing about the project is that during Knight's research, she has discovered the names of three soldiers who were previously thought lost, and though there is very little material about them, there was enough for Knight, secretary of the group, to have their names added to the Helston Memorial Plaque. Knight's drive and determination to work on this project was helped by her natural efficacy for research, due in part to her previous career in the police force, and by her love of the local community and our history.

The project began in 2014 with a small task force made up of members of the town council, including Knight, who wanted to do something particularly special to commemorate the beginning of the Great War. However, the task force decided early on that they would separate themselves from the town council in order to apply for charity funding for the project. They were successful and were eventually funded by the National Lottery, enough to be able to create exhibitions every November with the last one in 2018. The task force put together the first exhibition in the museum which focused on the beginning of the War and took place in a special exhibition room in the upstairs of the museum. It was obviously very successful during its one-month duration, and the people of the task force decided that they had barely scratched the surface of what they wanted to have in the primary exhibit. The following years saw the focus of the exhibition becoming about 'The War at Sea and In the Air' including airships, and 'The Home Front' which looked at the soldiers at home and the importance of the women of the war. This year's exhibition focuses on the return of soldiers from the First World War and the years immediately following the end of the conflict. In continuing the project, Knight insisted that once she began, she 'couldn't not finish', and that to do so would have been an injustice to those who lived through it. Today, she is the last member of the original task force, and this year's exhibition has been curated by her alone. She has, however, strongly stated the importance of the community in her creation of the exhibitions not just this year, but in all the years previously as well. Knight is a very prominent member of the local community, and thus many people have offered their family treasures and keepsakes to help with her exhibition. As an example, one gentleman gave her his grandfather's medals the day before it opened. One aspect of the community participation which is particularly prominent is the quilt that hangs in the main section of the museum. It is made up of sixty-two squares which each represent the sixty-two servicemen of Helston who died in the War and was created by forty different people who had varying levels of sewing skills. Knight was the individual who connected the squares and created the final product which hangs proudly above a scrapbook of who made the squares and what it personally means to them. Another commemorative event linked to the exhibition project is the bell ringing on the centenary of each soldier's death. The bells of St. Michael's church ring a hundred times to honour their sacrifice, a tradition which will continue until 2020, for the last soldier who passed away from war-related inflictions in 1920. As part of the community focus, the heritage project has run outreach events for local primary schools, where Knight has been discussing the project and the war in a broader sense to the children of Helston and the surrounding areas, some of whose ancestors fought in the conflict. Knight is also giving talks to museum visitors towards the end of November in the exhibition itself, as part of the outreach programme. An important event for the Heritage Project was the Flower Festival which took place in July 2017, and used floral displays created by the small businesses and individuals in the community in order to celebrate and educate thirty different aspects of World War One, with Knight providing the historical research and information. It was held in the Central Methodist Church on Coinage Street, close by the War Memorial, and encouraged not only members of the local community to gain more knowledge of the War and its remembrance, but holiday makers as well.

The exhibition space, as stated previously, is situated in a separate room above the main area of the museum. The room itself is L-shaped and used for temporary exhibitions such as this. For the 2017 exhibition, which focused on 'The Home Front' of Helston, the space was transformed into a flat that was stylised as a typical living space from that period, with a mannequin of a crying woman at a table, and another mannequin of a sick soldier in a bed and furniture donated by the local Helston community. This year, however, the space is more typical of a museum exhibition. Along the left side wall are posters of information of each year from 1918 to 1938. They detail the key events of local history and national history leading up to the beginning of the Second World War. The centre of the room consists of glass cases which showcase the flapper dresses of the Roaring Twenties and detail the attitudes and ideologies of that generation who were too young to fight in the Great War. It emphasises their desire to make the most of the lives their parents' generation had fought so hard and died for, and how they were affected by the consequences of the war. At the back of the room, Knight has displayed information of the men who served and survived and honoured them with as much information that she could find. Alongside the wall display is an easel which holds the framed Roll of

Honour of Helston. In some of the other glass cases are the medals, photographs and heirlooms of the local people of the time, donated by their descendants for the exhibition, and information about the history of each of the pieces. Finally, is what Knight affectionately calls the Miscellaneous Wall; the odds and ends of the research that doesn't seem to fit in any other category of the exhibition but is still an important aspect of remembrance. The most important information portrayed in the exhibition, however, is the explanation of the ending of the war, from Armistice to the completion of the effects of the Treaty of Versailles. Knight hopes that this exhibition portrays the sombre reality of the Great War and the scars it left on the country, but also that our town looked towards a bright future through community spirit, a spirit that Knight arguably has proved was as strong then as it is today.

Throughout her time on the Helston Heritage Project, Knight has also developed her own archival collection. She has collected original letters of soldiers to their loved ones, and recorded family members recounting the stories of their ancestors during war time, both at home and abroad. These stories vary in their voices, from a ten-year-old girl about her Great, Great Grandfather to relatives who were born soon after the war ended. The recordings were originally intended to be played at a historical celebration event in August 2017. Perhaps the greatest breakthrough of the project's research was the discovery of three more Helston soldiers who passed away during the War; they are Thomas J. Angove, John H. Richards and William J. Williams. Knight arranged for their names to be added to Helston's war memorial in honour of these brave men, but discovering their names was an unexpected surprise. She stated that most of the documentation of Helston's First World War, including details on servicemen, was destroyed during the Second World War. This caused a huge barrier to much of her research. However, the skills she developed from her former employment meant that she was able to uncover much of her information both through discussions and donations from members of the public, and through archival resources. But these soldiers may not be the last ones who she manages to name. She has a photograph of thirty-five soldiers returning from the War who remain unnamed and is appealing to the community once again for recognition or information about them. Though this is the final exhibition to take place in the museum, Knight and the town council are planning an event in June 2019, which commemorates the centenary of the signing of the Treaty of Versailles. In contrast to the sombre nature of November's remembrance and honour, June's event will be one of joy and celebration to emulate how the news was received in 1919 across Britain.

This year, Knight was honoured for her dedication to the Heritage Project by the British Legion. She was invited to the Peoples March in

London for this year's Armistice centenary Remembrance service and was invited to lay a wreath of poppies at the Cenotaph. On the wreath she attached the aforementioned sixty-two cards that represented Helston's fallen servicemen. She also had the chance to represent and honour her own family members who served and carried a photograph of her Great Grandfather in a frame along the march. On Saturday 10 November she also attended the Royal British Legion Festival of Remembrance at the Royal Albert Hall. She kept in contact with the Helston community throughout her time in London by updating the Helston World War One Heritage Projects' Facebook page with photographs of the events and how she felt being able to represent our community in such a beautiful way. She states that 'Nothing can describe the pride I have felt going to London to represent not only our project, but also some of my own family who served. It is a weekend that will never leave me and that I hope will inspire the younger generation to continue to remember when we too have passed by'.[4] This highlights the contemporary importance of social media in disseminating knowledge of past conflicts to younger generations.[5]

This summarises perfectly what the exhibition has meant to her both as an individual and as part of the group project. Her trip to London was also a way to represent everyone who helped with the project, from the small task force in the beginning to the community of volunteers and donators. This project has become an inspiration to those in the community who wish to honour our local heroes of World War One, and the brave men and women who are currently serving in our armed forces, including, if not especially, those at Culdrose Naval Base and Air Station. But this project is just as much about Knight herself as much as the people she honours in the exhibitions. As a volunteer, she has gone above and beyond to educate and inspire the local community and bring us together. She has praised the sacrifices of the servicemen from Helston and the surrounding parishes, acknowledged the technological feat of military engineers of the time and shone a light on the unsung heroes of West Cornwall.

NOTES AND REFERENCES

[1] For information on the wider activities of the Museum see www.museumofcornishlife.co.uk/ [last accessed 26 November 2018].
[2] The Museum's commemoration of the First World War in Helston should be considered in the context of wider Public Engagement throughout the United Kingdom and elsewhere on the subject. There have been a number of academic projects that have emerged over the past four years with the Arts and Humanities Research Council (AHRC) funding five Engagement Centres to bring together

researchers and community groups:
www.ahrc.ukri.org/research/fundedthemesandprogrammes/worldwaroneanditslega
cy/worldwaroneengagementcentres/ [last accessed 26 November 2018]. Another
interesting project, also funded by the AHRC, is entitled 'Reflections on the
Centenary of the First World War' and it seeks to explore different aspects of this
'academic-public engagement': www.reflections1418.exeter.ac.uk/ [last accessed
26 November 2018].

[3] Much of the information for this review article was collected during a fieldwork
visit to the Museum of Cornish Life at Helston on 31 October 2018.

[4] www.facebook.com/Helstonww1heritageproject [last accessed on 19 November
2018]

[5] For another example of a First World War project that used social media see
'Richard Charles Graves-Sawle: Great War Cornish Soldier'. This was an initiative
in 2014 of Emily Poole and Ellie Vale, two Public History students associated with
the Institute of Cornish Studies, who used twitter to make extracts of Richard's
wartime diary available to the general public:
www.greatwarcornishsoldier.exeter.ac.uk/ [last accessed on 27 November 2018]

NOTES ON CONTRIBUTORS

Froshie Evans is an MPhil/PhD candidate with the Institute of Cornish Studies who is conducting a comparative study of Cornish and Welsh storytelling. She has a BA (Hons) and an MA in Film and Television Studies from Falmouth University. Although she comes from an academic background of culture and storytelling, she is interested in the history of Cornwall, particularly of West Cornwall. She lives in Helston; a recent move having grown up in Falmouth. This is where she first heard of Martine Knight's Helston World War One project and she decided that her contribution was to review the project for Cornwall and the Great War. She is assisting in the development of the cultural and community history projects of the Institute's Agan Kernow programme.

Melanie James is an academic historian and editor. She is founder and owner of 'Take it as read' (www.takeitasread.com), a complete writing service. Melanie has an MA in British First World War Studies from the University of Birmingham, where her dissertation focused on the early Cornish response to the declaration of war in 1914 for which she gained a Distinction. She also has an MBA from the University of Lancaster, a graduate Diploma in International Marketing Management from Boston University, Brussels, and a BA (Hons) in French from the University of Warwick. Melanie now lives in Sussex but was born in Plymouth, Devon. She has a strong interest in Cornwall where her family are recorded living in Breage in the 1500s.

Victoria Jenner is a former student associated with the Institute of Cornish Studies and in recent years has been contributing towards its digital development programme as an Associate Graduate Researcher. Victoria's interest in Cornwall's society and economy has influenced her research into the changing identities of micro-communities in Cornwall, especially those that have centred on industrial turned tourist dependent narratives. Now Victoria acts as consultant to the Institute's Cornish Maritime Churches project, whilst working for the National Trust as a digital curator specialising in 18th century socio-political history.

Alan M. Kent was born in Cornwall and graduated from the Universities of Cardiff and Exeter, specialising in Celtic and Anglo-Celtic literatures. For several years he worked as a teacher and now lectures in Literature for the Open University and is Visiting Fellow in Celtic Studies at the University of La Coruña, Galicia. In addition to writing novels, he has published a number of prize-winning plays and volumes of poetry. As well as his non-fiction writing, he has also edited several collections of Cornish and Anglo-Cornish Literature. He is the series editor of 'Lesser Used Languages of Europe', literary editor of 'Corpus Textorum Cornicorum' and joint series editor of 'Cornish and Celtic Alternatives'. His latest books include Interim Nation (2015), Dan Daddow's Cornish Comicalities (2016) and The Festivals of Cornwall: Ritual, Revival, Reinvention (2018).

Philip Payton is Emeritus Professor of Cornish and Australian Studies at the University of Exeter, and Professor of History at Flinders University in Adelaide, Australia. Recent books include The Maritime History of Cornwall (ed. with Alston Kennerley and Helen Doe) (2014), Australia in the Great War (2015), One and All: Labor and the Radical Tradition in South Australia (2016), Emigrants and Historians: Essays in Honour of Eric Richards (ed., 2016), A History of Sussex (2017), Cornwall: A History (revised edition, 2017), and 'Repat': A Concise History of Repatriation in Australia (2018). At present he is preparing a revised edition of his The Cornish Overseas: A History of Cornwall's 'Great Emigration' and is editing a collection Cornwall in the Age of Rebellion, both to be published during 2019 by University of Exeter Press.

34261025R00074

Printed in Poland
by Amazon Fulfillment
Poland Sp. z o.o., Wrocław